STATISTICAL SAMPLING
RISK ANALYSIS IN AUDITING

Other books for auditors by Peter Jones:

Combating Fraud and Corruption in the Public Sector, 1993, Chapman&Hall, London, ISBN 0 412 46370 9

P C Jones and J G Bates, *Public Sector Auditing – practical techniques for an integrated approach*, 2nd Edn, 1994, Chapman&Hall, London, ISBN 0 412 56500 5

Statistical Sampling and Risk Analysis in Auditing

Peter Jones

Routledge
Taylor & Francis Group

LONDON AND NEW YORK

First published 1999 by Gower Publishing

Published 2017 by Routledge
2 Park Square, Milton Park, Abingdon, Oxfordshire OX14 4RN
711 Third Avenue, New York, NY 10017, USA

First issued in paperback 2017

Routledge is an imprint of the Taylor & Francis Group, an informa business

British Library Cataloguing in Publication Data
Jones, Peter
  Statistical sampling and risk analysis in auditing
  1. Auditing – Statistical methods 2. Sampling (Statistics)
  I. Title
  657.4'5

Library of Congress Cataloging-in-Publication Data
Jones, Peter, 1947–
  Statistical sampling and risk analysis in auditing/Peter Jones.
    p. cm.
  Includes index.
  ISBN 0–566–08080–X (hardcover)
  1. Auditing–Statistical methods. 2. Sampling (Statistics)
  I. Title.
  HF5667.J66 1998
  657'.45–dc21

Typeset in 11/13pt Palatino by Wearset, Boldon, Tyne and Wear.

ISBN 13: 978-1-138-26321-5 (pbk)
ISBN 13: 978-0-566-08080-7 (hbk)

Contents

List of figures   ix
List of tables   x
List of case studies   xi

1 Introduction   1
The people this book aims to help   1
The help on offer   2
Reading through and getting the most from this book   3
Recent developments   4
Conclusion   5

2 Statistical and non-statistical approaches   7
Is there really a lot of difference between statistical and
non-statistical?   7
Main approaches   11
    Haphazard   11
    Judgmental (selective)   12
    Equal interval (or systematic)   13
    Statistical   14
Conclusion

3 Why bother to use statistical sampling?
Professional standards
Increasing the value of your audit
  Testing
  Taking account of risk and materiality
  Independence
  Speed and efficiency
  Making optimal use of information technology
  Accountability and audit management
Potential pitfalls and disadvantages
  The need for planning
  Cost of investing in new skills
  An unrealistic sense of security
Conclusion

4 Theory, concepts and conditions
Probability
The normal distribution
Precision, confidence and point estimates
The reliability factor
  The population
  The population characteristic
  Sampling units
  Access to the sample (sampling frames)
Errors
Random (or known chance) selection
Conclusion

5 Attribute sampling
Attribute sample size
Sampling interval
Case study 1: compliance testing during a stock system
audit
Suggestions
Case study 2: compliance testing a purchases system
Conclusion

6 An introduction to monetary unit sampling (MUS) 51
Substantive or compliance testing and the role of MUS 51
The purpose and pitfalls of MUS 53
  Sample size and sampling interval for MUS 54
  Some initial precautions 55
Case study 3: external audit of year-end creditor's figure 57
Suggestions 57
Case study 4: the internal audit of a creditor's
payment system 60
Suggestions 60
Conclusion 64

7 Monetary unit sampling – taking account of errors 67
Two options 67
The safety margin and precision gap widening 68
The mechanics of extrapolation 70
  Three main stages of MUS extrapolation 70
Case study 5: MUS with overpayment error 75
Case study 6: MUS overpayments extrapolated beyond
MTEL 76
Case study 7: MUS with over- and underpayment error 82
Conclusion 83

8 Risk models and the reduction of sample sizes 87
Risk of what? 89
A simple triangular relationship 90
Using 'nightmare' scenarios to identify key risks 91
Typical key control questions – purchasing system 93
The total audit risk model 94
Case study 8: too much work! 96
Case study 9: taking account of wider audit evidence 98
Suggestions 100
Conclusion 104

9 Other sampling approaches 107
Acceptance sampling 107
Combined sample size for attribute and MUS 110
Variables sampling 111

Mean per unit sampling   111
Ratio estimation   112
Difference estimation   112
Conclusion   114

10 Final concluding thoughts   115
How should I introduce statistical sampling to my audit?   115

Appendices   121
1   Additional case studies   123
2   Glossary   141
3   Abbreviations   147
4   SAS 430   149
5   Tables   161
6   Further reading   166

Index   169

List of figures

2.1   Relationship between sample size and reliability   9

4.1   Normal distribution   30

7.1   Precision gap widening   69

7.2(a) MUS Evaluation Sheet   72

7.2(b) MUS Evaluation Sheet   78

7.2(c) MUS Evaluation Sheet   80

7.2(d) MUS Evaluation Sheet   84

8.1   Objectives, risks and controls   90

8.2   Effect of overpayment   102

Appendices

Worksheet 1   136

Worksheet 2   138

List of tables

1.1 Recent developments   5

3.1 SAS 430: Basic principles and essential procedures   19

4.1 Reliability factors   33

9.1 Acceptance sampling   108

9.2 Estimated upper error limits (UELs) to nearest whole percentage from compliance testing   110

Appendices

4   Table 1 Some factors influencing sample size for tests of controls   158

  Table 2 Some factors influencing sample size for substantive tests   159

5   Table 1 Random numbers   163

  Table 2 Cumulative poisson probabilities   164

List of case studies

1 Compliance testing during a stock system audit   41

2 Compliance testing a purchases system   46

3 External audit of year-end creditor's figure   57

4 The internal audit of a creditor's payment system   60

5 MUS with overpayment error   75

6 MUS overpayments extrapolated beyond MTEL   76

7 MUS with over- and underpayment error   82

8 Too much work!   96

9 Taking account of wider audit evidence   98

1 Introduction

The people this book aims to help

This book is for people responsible for managing or undertaking audits. Both internal and external audits can benefit from statistical sampling and both have been borne in mind throughout. A reasonable level of audit experience is assumed, though little or no experience or knowledge of statistics or statistical sampling methods is expected. The book may well be useful to directors, members of audit committees and others who, while they might not be directly involved in auditing, are concerned about various strategic aspects such as the cost of the audit, the amount of audit testing and the overall coverage of important systems.

Although the book makes no attempt to cover any academic or professional syllabus, students of accounting, auditing and others whose courses include auditing will also find the book useful.

We have tried to keep the text to a length suitable for people who are more interested in how to start applying statistical sampling in practical, financial auditing than in knowing every possible sampling technique, every application and the derivation of every formula.

The help on offer

Our main concern is to help professional auditors decide when and how best to use statistical sampling during their ordinary work. Although this is not a book about statistics, and in most situations auditors will not need to become statisticians, some explanation of statistical concepts and theory is unavoidable, although this has been kept as far as possible to a useful minimum. We have sometimes pointed out when further advice might be needed, though readers must decide for themselves, within the limitless variation of possible practical situations, exactly when to seek specialist statistical advice.

Despite the enormous and ever-expanding range of audits faced in modern organizations, certain widely-applicable sampling approaches can be discerned and it is upon these that we concentrate. Statistical sampling owes its steadily increasing popularity among auditors to many sources, but four stand out:

1   Existing publications, some of which are listed in Appendix 6.
2   Reasonably well-established practice among external auditing firms and the National Audit Office.
3   Increasing use of, and training in, statistical sampling among internal auditors.
4   Auditing standards and guidance from professional bodies.

This book has not attempted to follow any particular one of the sources just mentioned above. Rather, we have tried to utilize the best suggestions and influences from each, plus any other ideas and practical points that help auditors plan and manage their work to achieve typical audit objectives.

For example, some typical questions that arise and for which help is often sought include the following, though in no particular order or priority:

- How many items should we test?
- What should we do if we are not certain how many items we are sampling from?

- Do we select samples differently for compliance and substantive tests?
- What should we take into account during our audit planning?
- Do we need to test items in a different way, or alter our audit programmes?
- Can we take into account our risk assessments/models?
- How do we extrapolate results from samples to the system/account being audited?
- What are the most convenient formulas?
- What sort of standard working papers might we use?
- How confident of our conclusions can we be?
- Should we involve our clients in our approach?
- Can we report our statistical results in a straightforward manner?
- Is this going to cost a lot of money for training, software and such?

These and many more practical queries will arise when auditors introduce, or expand their use of, statistical sampling. While we can not promise to offer the perfect solution to every conceivable problem, our emphasis on the practical difficulties and the most commonly used approaches should help you to work out a solution for your particular audits. The basic principles and direction of thought should be clear to you as the book progresses, and these will be illustrated by case studies to help clarify detailed techniques in realistic situations.

Reading through and getting the most from this book

Chapters 2, 3 and 4 are, unavoidably, rather discursive: Chapter 2 sets statistical sampling in a wider audit sampling context for the benefit of the complete newcomer; Chapter 3 looks at the advantages and disadvantages; and Chapter 4 looks at some of the basic theory. If you are already reasonably familiar with these aspects, particularly the theory, you may find it worthwhile to delve straight in to Chapter 5 on attribute sampling.

If, as is often the case whenever one approaches new ideas, some of the principles and techniques seem a little complex on first reading, it may help to work through the cases before rereading the theory. In fact, reading back and forward between the explanatory text and the cases is often the best approach. Some people find it easier to read and reflect upon the former, while others find it easier to work through the latter, but both are recommended.

The case studies are accompanied by suggested solutions. These suggestions are not 'cast in tablets of stone'. It may well be that you have greater or fewer resources than those assumed in the case and may wish to offer more or less assurance to your auditees. It is often possible to rework a case with your assumptions built in.

Do not be too concerned if at first you feel that some of the more complex aspects could not realistically be adopted for your range of audits. Increasing familiarity with statistical sampling techniques is like increasing familiarity with many other things – it's surprising what hidden benefits can arise. Perhaps the secret of successfully applying these techniques in your complex professional environment is to proceed cautiously – an incremental approach, gaining confidence yourselves and gradually bringing others, including auditees, on board. A good way to begin gaining experience is often to use attribute sampling when testing internal controls, as we will see in due course. These points are reconsidered in Chapter 10.

Recent developments

The development of statistical sampling techniques in auditing has an interesting history, but one beyond the scope of this book. We have, however, provided a brief table of some of the important landmarks for the benefit of those who feel more comfortable with an historical context. (A list of abbreviations is given in Appendix 3.)

Table 1.1   Recent developments

- 1960s – Professional guidance papers on this topic issued by the AICPA in the USA.

- 1970 – IMTA (now CIPFA) issued a small volume titled Statistical Sampling in Auditing.

- During the late 1970s and the 1980s a number of published works appeared on both sides of the Atlantic, written mainly by learned academics and professional bodies such as the ICAEW and the AICPA, some of which are mentioned in Appendix 6. During this time the use of statistical sampling appears to have increased among the major accounting firms and been taken on board by the National Audit Office.

- 1981 – AICPA in the USA issued statement on auditing standard SAS 39 entitled Audit Sampling.

- 1987 – The APC (now APB) issued an exposure draft guideline entitled Audit Sampling. This exposure draft was accompanied by an 'Audit Brief' offering relatively detailed guidance on techniques and examples of possible applications. Both these documents remained in circulation for consultation until 1995.

- During the early 1990s a survey done by CIPFA indicated a growing interest and use of statistical sampling methods by internal audit departments in the UK.

- 1995 – The APB in the UK issued its long-awaited guideline SAS 430, entitled Audit Sampling, setting the standard expected of all CCAB auditors during '... any audit using sampling ...'. This guideline comments upon both statistical and non-statistical approaches.

- 1996 (December) – The IFA's IAPC issued an exposure draft entitled Audit Sampling and Other Selective Testing Procedures.

Note: USA and UK SASs are not a single series of standards.

Conclusion

This book is about the value of statistical sampling to the practical side of auditing. It is written for auditors by an experienced auditor, who is familiar with statistical sampling in both external and internal audit situations.

A range of situations and questions will be addressed, but you should not worry at this stage if some of the more complicated scenarios seem to lack immediate relevance to your own work. It is often more efficient to build up your approach to sampling as you gain experience, rather than try to introduce across-the-board changes to all your audits.

In relatively recent times interest in this topic has grown rapidly throughout the profession. Standards have been promulgated by various professional bodies that imply all auditors should be aware of statistical sampling techniques and know when these should be used.

2   Statistical and non-statistical approaches

In this chapter we consider the position of statistical sampling in relation to the wider question of how to go about selecting items to test during an audit.

Is there really a lot of difference between statistical and non-statistical?

At first it might seem so. Opinions are often divided between those who use statistical sampling and those who reject it. In 1991 a survey of a wide variety of organizations undertaken on behalf of CIPFA indicated that there was a growing interest in the use of statistical sampling. Any distinct split between acceptance and rejection was less pronounced than had at first been expected.

It is often convenient to think in terms of a broad division between statistical and non-statistical approaches, which sometimes gives rise to people reserving the term 'sampling' exclusively for statistical sampling and referring to non-statistical approaches as 'selection'. A sharp division between 'statistical'

7

and 'non-statistical' is understandable in workplace conversation, particularly when talking broadly about, say, your audit strategy for the next three years or your approach to testing a particular system or account. But when we get down to the level of particular audits and test programmes, it is often more helpful to bear in mind that we are usually talking about a range of possible approaches to sampling and that both statistical and non-statistical approaches can actually have a lot in common.

Professional judgment lies behind and underpins all audit sampling. There is a myth perpetuated in some circles that statistical sampling in some way relieves the auditor of the need to use professional judgment – 'everything will depend upon formula' – but nothing could be further from the truth.

Both statistical and non-statistical sampling aim to help the auditor form a conclusion covering the whole population, that is, including the rest of the items not sampled. (If all the items of a particular type are selected because of a particular characteristic not possessed by the rest of the population, then this is not usually called a sample – for example, all vouchers processed by a particular employee known to have been a fraudster.)

There is always a probability, or risk, of forming the wrong conclusion in either approach. Clearly, as the number of items sampled increases, or if the wording of the conclusion itself is made less demanding, the risk of being wrong is lessened. But unless all, or nearly all, items are sampled, or the conclusions are very undemanding, there will be some risk that the conclusion arrived at will be incorrect.

Perhaps the relationship between the risk of forming the wrong conclusion (in practical terms this is usually the risk of missing something important during your testing) and the amount of testing in relation to the whole population is more easily apparent from the following Figure 2.1

Whether you plan to sample on a statistical basis or not, the more you test, the less will be the risk of any given conclusion being wrong but, ultimately, these parameters depend on your professional judgment as to what is acceptable in terms of risk, that is, how reliable you want your results to be and how accurate a conclusion you wish to make.

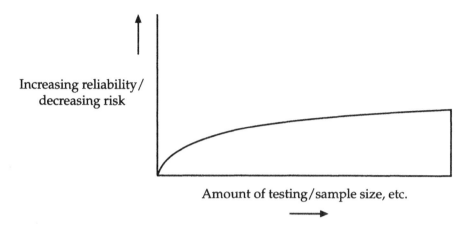

Increasing reliability/
decreasing risk

Amount of testing/sample size, etc.

Figure 2.1   Relationship between sample size and reliability

Consider a simple example and some questions that it raises:

- If, say, from 15 000 invoices you just picked the first convenient 1 000 and tested them for proper authorization, how reliable would your results be and what conclusion could you draw if you found none that were improperly authorized?
- If you found nothing wrong, on a non-statistical basis would you perhaps conclude that 'all invoices were likely to be properly authorized'? Or that 'we felt invoice authorization was reliably performed'?
- Would not your conclusion rather depend on how typical of the rest of the invoices you felt your sample to be?
- Would you not need to consider the order in which the invoices had been picked? Did convenience mean that only ones for the first month of a year were picked, or the first few letters of the alphabet, or the first few cost codes? Or was it 'convenient' at the time to pick items in a way that avoided any significant bias?
- Even if no errors were found in this case, what is the chance of a sample of this size including any errors if, say, the real error rate was 1 in 10 000? Or, say, 1 in 100?
- A sample size of 1 000 would seem rather large to some

people. What if only 10 had been sampled compared to what you thought was the likely error rate in the whole population of invoices?

- Perhaps the first question you would ask is, 'what sort of error rate should I worry about in the first place?'

These are the sorts of question that auditors are almost bound to encounter. An experienced auditor will be able to make some fairly shrewd guesses and professional judgments, depending on what information is available about the population and the systems controlling it.

With the use of statistical methods, however, many of the ordinary questions likely to be asked, particularly at the planning stage of an audit, can be used to derive quantifiable statements and conclusions that generally give far better value from any particular audit sample, provided it is selected and analysed according to some fairly basic rules.

So, going back to the question at the start of this chapter, in one sense the answer is no, insofar as both statistical and non-statistical approaches are generally concerned to arrive at similar conclusions and both raise similar questions. But when it comes to ways of answering such questions and forming professional conclusions, that is, the detailed methods of selection and evaluation, the answer is usually yes.

The three vital ingredients for most conclusions, which we shall return to again later on, are:

1   What is my estimate of error (or control deviation, or other characteristic of the account or system)?
2   How confident am I about this estimate?
3   How precise a statement can I make about my estimate?

Statistical sampling offers the more reliable way of stating these conclusions within reasonable measures, but before we go on to consider this aspect in more detail and some of the other advantages and disadvantages of statistical sampling, let's compare some of the main terms used to classify types of statistical and non-statistical approaches.

Main approaches

Popular classifications typically divide sampling into four broad approaches based on the method used to select the items in the sample; haphazard, judgmental (or selective), equal interval or (systematic) and statistical. Unfortunately these terms are often used rather loosely, overlapping between statistical and non-statistical sampling, and this can cause confusion, so we will spend a little time considering what is meant by each.

Haphazard

This approach is sometimes taken to mean that the auditor gives no thought to how items are selected, perhaps picking a few vouchers easily in reach from shelves stacked with thousands. It is difficult to think of many situations in which this approach is justified. An auditor might pick a few items in this haphazard way when attempting to learn about a new system, or perhaps to confirm something that he or she has just been told.

'Haphazard' is also used to mean that the auditor makes a deliberate effort to avoid any obvious bias when items are selected, perhaps picking a voucher or two more evenly from each shelf. In fact, any auditor is likely to be subject to influences that are difficult to pin down and avoid: perhaps one person might tend to avoid vouchers that are rather difficult to reach; perhaps some shelves contain irrelevant papers hidden between the vouchers; or one might not be aware of a tendency to avoid part of a sequence in which items are stored, such as the last letters of the alphabet. A haphazard sample in this sense of the word is also difficult to justify for most audit testing, as one cannot usually know in advance if it is indicative of the rest of the items from which it was chosen or of any special concerns such as items likely to be fraudulent.

However, it is only fair to point out that SAS 430 (see Appendix 4), an important standard that we shall consider further, indicates (para. 22) that haphazard sampling '... may be an acceptable alternative to random selection provided auditors are satisfied that the sample is representative of the entire population'. It is the provision that is so very difficult to be confident about, because, to be satisfied that the sample is representative of the population on an haphazard basis, an auditor will usually need to select a rather large sample, or to know so much in detail about the population that one is left to wonder why a sample was selected for audit evidence in the first place. Indeed, in the very next sentence the standard warns auditors of the need to be cautious when relying on this approach.

Judgmental (selective)

This term is perhaps the most loosely used of all. Few auditors would admit to choosing a sample without using their judgment and so almost any sample can be called judgmental. Indeed, the auditor relies on judgment if it is claimed that a haphazard sample will be representative of the population when the haphazard approach is used.

Judgmental sampling often refers to a variety of ways of dividing the population prior to the final selection of items, for example, dividing it into sub-populations of different value items, or strata, and sampling each one separately (stratified sampling), or dividing a population of internal control events into time periods such as months or weeks and ensuring each period is sampled. In this way judgmental is simply a stage in one of the other categories of sampling. Unfortunately a 'judgmental' sample can sometimes be an excuse for not thinking through all the implications of the actual selection process. How many items should you pick from each strata or time period? On what basis, statistical or non-statistical?

Clearly, judgmental sampling can encompass a range of possibilities, from sampling that is little more sophisticated than the simplest of haphazard selection but does attempt to incorporate some element of professional judgment, to more sophisticated regimes that incorporate different statistical (and non-statistical) plans for different strata or for clusters in the population.

Judgmental sampling is also sometimes used to refer to a sample that is deliberately 'biased', in that it attempts to select items that the auditor already knows or suspects will not be typical of the population. This is often no more than simply subdividing the main population to target, say, periods of known lapses in internal control, or items suspected of fraudulent treatment, though, if the sub-population is tested in its entirety, it is of course no longer being sampled.

Sometimes a sample may be selected randomly, in a similar fashion to a statistical sample, but not evaluated on a statistical basis. This tends to cause further confusion among those who (wrongly) equate any random selection with statistical sampling, when in fact a non-statistical judgmental evaluation took place. It is perhaps more useful to refer to such a sample as 'random judgmental'.

Although judgmental sampling in one form or another is a fairly common approach, it is an unfortunate term because it tends to be more associated with non-statistical approaches, implying that statistical approaches somehow reduce the role of professional judgment, when in fact the reverse is usually true, as we shall see.

Equal interval (or systematic)
Here the auditor simply divides the population into equally measured intervals and starts by selecting one item from the first interval, another from an equal distance into the next interval, and so on, choosing perhaps an item that falls in the middle of each interval or at the beginning or the end. By making each interval between items selected equal, one attempts to reduce the risk of bias. Thus, if one wanted a sample of 10 from a population of 10 000 and the first item sampled was number 320, the second would be number 1 320, and so on, to number 9 320.

One step on from this would be to select the first item on a random basis (from between 1 and 1 000 in the foregoing example) further reducing the likelihood of bias. For most situations an auditor can assume that an equal interval selection from a random start is random, that is, each item has an equal chance of being selected.

One point of caution: if the first number happens to hit a pattern in the population, this randomness will be compromised.

If, say, all supervisors' payslips in a weekly payroll were processed first and a low number was selected at the start, then only or nearly only supervisors would be selected. It may be worth guarding against such a possibility by examining the population in more detail before testing or picking more than one random start. If two random starts had been picked from the population of 10 000 mentioned above, say 320 and 1 794, each item would generate a sequence 2 000 greater – 2 320, 3 794, and so on – to still end up with a sample of 10 items.

A slight variation on the equal interval selection, sometimes called 'cell selection', is when each item is selected randomly from within each equal interval, or cell. As long as an equal proportion of the sample is selected from cells of equal size, randomness is still maintained, otherwise one has a form of stratified sampling.

Obviously, equal-interval selection can be used during either statistical or non-statistical sampling.

Statistical

Given the tendency for terms to be used rather loosely and for sampling to gradually increase in sophistication, what then distinguishes a statistical from a non-statistical sample? Basically, statistical sampling follows the laws of probability theory, whereas non-statistical sampling does not. In practical terms this boils down to ensuring:

- that all items of the population (and hence in the sample) have an equal or known chance of selection, which is why random selection is so commonly used, as it ensures that bias is avoided;
- that the sample results were evaluated mathematically according to probability theory, though this does not necessarily mean that only one possible evaluation can be made from one set of results.

Three broad types of statistical sampling are listed below, and of these the first two are currently far more likely to be used for financial auditing and demand most of our attention in this book.

1 Attribute sampling.
2 Probability proportional to size sampling (usually in the form of monetary unit sampling).
3 Variables sampling.

Before we go on to look at these in later chapters and given our comments upon non-statistical approaches, let's first consider some advantages and disadvantages. Indeed, why bother with statistical sampling?

Conclusion

Statistical and non-statistical approaches to audit sampling are not two mutually exclusive alternatives. Rather, different combinations are possible within a range of sampling techniques that auditors should use, depending on which, in their professional judgment, best meets:

- the audit objectives;
- the resources at their disposal;
- professional guidance (where appropriate).

For most audit objectives the conclusions from testing, for which statistical sampling tends to be particularly well suited, will be critical.

3 Why bother to use statistical sampling?

This chapter considers the advantages and disadvantages of statistical sampling for auditors, together with some of the key decisions and potential pitfalls. A chapter of reasonable length cannot hope to be complete in its coverage of these important factors, and it would often be misleading to simply list the 'for' and 'against' points, because so much depends on the context in which each occurs. Rather, we have chosen issues that are important to most auditors and for which the approach to sampling is likely to be of concern.

Professional standards

We have already mentioned these in passing. The general trend towards catering for statistical sampling in professional auditing standards in the UK and the USA is apparent from Table 1.1, though in both countries exposure drafts and various other publications not included in this table have been issued from time to time. Although these standards have been issued by professional accountancy bodies, individual auditors, particularly internal auditors, do not come exclusively from an accountancy background. Other bodies such as the IIA, the BSI and many academics have published excellent contributions, and some of these are listed in Appendix 6. Nevertheless, in this country, like most of the rest of the world, auditing still tends to be dominated by accountants, and for the sake of reasonable brevity we shall limit our consideration accordingly.

In the UK the main standard is currently SAS 430, issued by the APB, see Appendix 4, though the guidance issued by the (then) APC during the period of the exposure draft and by the CIPFA following SAS 430 are particularly helpful. (See Appendix 6 for details.)

Important though these pronouncements are, it would be unhelpful for auditors to rely solely on professional standards when considering the rationale for statistical sampling. Few attitudes are more likely to lose the confidence of auditees, or one's own colleagues, than unquestioning adherence to a set of 'rules' issued by some remote third party. Indeed SAS 430 seems to discourage this attitude at various points by drawing attention to the choices open to auditors and the need for professional judgment.

Perhaps the most helpful reason for taking account of such professional standards, though it sounds a little negative at first, is to minimize the opportunity for subsequent criticism. Hindsight is the bane of many an auditor's efforts: auditors are accused of relying on it when they point out that auditees might have benefited from following various standards of best practice and they will lay themselves doubly open to subsequent criticism if they fail to do the same! At the very least it is both useful and professional to be clear in one's own mind about the reasons for not following a relevant professional standard.

The general trend of SAS 430 can seem a little uneven at times. It tends to mix the definition of terms with selective comments on what auditors do, or may do. It can be helpful to read through the basic principles and essential procedures which form the actual standard (printed in bold in the text of the SAS) and think carefully about these, before reading the whole standard from start to finish. For convenience these are reproduced below.

Table 3.1 SAS 430: Basic principles and essential procedures

'430.1 When using either statistical or non-statistical sampling methods, auditors should design and select an audit sample, perform audit procedures thereon and evaluate sample results so as to obtain appropriate audit evidence.

430.2 When designing the size and structure of an audit sample, auditors should consider the specific audit objectives, the nature of the population from which they wish to sample, and the sampling and selection methods.

430.3 When determining sample sizes, auditors should consider sampling risk, the amount of error that would be acceptable and the extent to which they expect to find errors.

430.4 Auditors should select sample items in such a way that the sample can be expected to be representative of the population in respect of the characteristics being tested.

430.5 Having carried out, on each sample item, those audit procedures which are appropriate to the particular audit objective, auditors should:
  (a) analyse any errors detected in the sample; and
  (b) draw inferences for the population as a whole.'

Quoted by kind permission of the copyright holder, the CCAB.

At first these might seem to state the obvious, but on reflection one is bound to ask: how, exactly, can I prove that my selection of items and evaluation of findings achieves the above? Although a range of options is open, it becomes increasingly clear as the standard progresses that some form of statistical sampling is likely to be required, or at least to be well worth considering. All the considerations prompted by the standard tend to form a documented stage of a typical statistical sampling plan, and the standard as a whole tends to guide the auditor to a more professional approach to sampling (statistical and non-statistical) than might otherwise have been used.

Increasing the value of your audit

Testing
Among the procedures implied from a reading of SAS 430 is that auditors will make reasonable attempts to explore the implications of sample findings for the population as a whole.

In most non-statistical analysis it is difficult to draw any concrete inferences or extrapolations, certainly in any quantifiable or defensible manner. Sometimes the auditor will hit upon errors that arise from a recurring miscoding, misinterpretation of regulation or other underlying cause and be able to infer that all similar items in the population will be in error. Usually, though, drawing reliable inferences is not so straightforward. On a non-statistical basis auditors often have to fall back on their experience or 'judgment', but in an unstructured manner. Typical comments include:

'... one error, probably a one-off slip-up ...'

'... we didn't find anything wrong, so we'd better assume everything is fine ...'

'... we seem to have spotted a few more deviations than expected but the managers don't seem to think it's significant.'

'... I wonder if we should do a larger sample ...'

It's not that statistical samples involve fewer questions, but rather that one has a structured and more reliable way of putting these, and of interpreting the answers. This is particularly valuable for the audited client managers, or auditees, who also have to make sense of what the auditors are saying.

At first managers may be reassured if auditors find few or apparently insignificant errors, but inevitably this will eventually bring in to question the value of audits 'that don't find much'. Auditors will, of course, point out the value of other work such as suggestions for system improvement, management-style projects and VFM work. But even reasonably sound systems contain risk and usually some level of error. Here the performance of routine audits, particularly internal ones, comes under increasing pressure from resource-conscious managers. Such managers may jump to the defence of their staff, putting the most favourable interpretation possible on any errors: '... the auditors were here all week – if they only found two unsigned vouchers and a total of five pounds in error, things must be okay whatever they say in their report . . .'. The regular, and often unavoidable, reporting of minor errors and occasional control deviations tends to induce a negative feeling towards auditing.

This bad feeling can be compounded when auditors (understandably, perhaps) refuse to put their reputation on the line and say whether or not the conclusion amounts to a 'clean bill of health', or how much assurance the audit does offer, or some other definite measured statement of what the audit findings imply for the system, balances or other object of their testing. Short, and almost impossible to challenge, conclusions can give a false sense of security to anyone reading the audit report (this has been a longstanding problem with external audits), and may eventually lead to a disdainful reaction from among the more senior people on audit committees and at board level.

The critical advantage of statistical sampling is that it can offer a means of extrapolating errors, including the implications of nil errors, to the larger population in a quantitative and usually more reliable manner than would otherwise be possible. The key advantage of being able to measure the risk of relying on the sample helps auditors express more meaningful inferences, often for large and complex systems. The need for caution still remains, but the auditor does not have to be mealy-mouthed and defensive about findings that on a non-statistical basis can look quite unimpressive in themselves.

One particular advantage of monetary unit sampling (an approach considered in Chapter 7) is its ability to favour selection of higher value amounts, reducing the risk of a single large error, or a small number of large errors hidden among the items, ruining the auditor's conclusions. This can often be a worrying situation when faced with a large population of 'acceptable-looking' transactions.

It is usually more helpful to be able to agree testing parameters (we will discuss parameters in the next chapter) with managers, in advance of the audit, if possible. But, in any event, measured assurance offers auditors the opportunity to conclude in writing that a system operates to agreed parameters, or to state estimates of maximum projected error rates or values, or whatever measures suit the circumstances. These conclusions are usually a lot more valuable to hard-pressed clients than listing a few control deviations or a few pounds' worth of errors. This is particularly so when, as so often happens, such lists relate to huge balances or systems that handle millions of transactions.

There are other ways in which the value of audit testing can be increased when it is practical to use statistical sampling but, as these relate to a range of issues other than the fundamental point of testing, we shall consider them under separate headings.

Taking account of risk and materiality

Almost by definition haphazard sampling generally takes little account of risk. Risk and materiality can be taken into account on a judgmental basis depending on the judgments used to select the sample. As we shall see when we come to consider sampling techniques in more detail, particularly monetary unit sampling and risk in Chapters 7 and 8, statistical sampling tends to lend itself to accommodating certain risk models. It also has the advantage of focusing attention on the way risk is taken into account in sampling, even if no formal risk model is used. This can be particularly useful at the planning stage when perceived risk is a major determinant of audit effort, sample size and cost.

Independence

Always a potential source of conflict, the issue of independence can be clarified by the use of statistical sampling techniques. At the very least the auditor can point to the lack of bias in random or other statistical selection methods. Unfortunately, the apparent objectivity of statistical sampling might be used by some to divert attention away from subjective judgments about the statistical sample parameters, or the selective manner of subsequent analysis. But such threats to the auditor's independence will remain, irrespective of the sampling approach. At least the statistical approach encourages a clear statement of such judgmental elements. Perhaps it is wise to remember the old saying about 'lies, damned lies and statistics'.

Speed and efficiency

The speed and efficiency of statistical compared to non-statistical approaches will depend largely on your audit objectives and any particular test objectives arising from these. If your objectives are simple and/or lack rigour, a statistical sample may not be efficient. Perhaps a small balance or minor subsystem that requires testing but does not have a large transaction throughput could be examined sufficiently to satisfy most auditors' objectives, using a small judgmental sample or analytical review techniques. Perhaps your audit will require small judgmental samples from different unrelated activities, or you may feel you can perform a haphazard sample. The critical question is: what does your objective imply in terms of testing?

Often the answer points to testing large volumes of transactions or control events and reasonably rigorous conclusions, and then statistical sampling tends to become more speedy and efficient than other approaches.

Making optimal use of information technology

Without wishing to overemphasize the point, it is worth commenting that an increasing range and sophistication of software is available for using statistical sampling in an auditing context. Sampling techniques lend themselves to highly computerized transaction-processing systems, payroll, creditors, stock control, claims processing, and so on. Most auditors can utilize statistical sampling to great effect once the principles are understood, as explained in this book, and some time is spent becoming familiar with particular applications.

Accountability and audit management

Earlier comments on extrapolation have already indicated the increased potential for statistical sampling to enhance accountability to audit committees and, by implication, the strategic management of audit. This is particularly so, for example, when offering assurance about the operation of main financial systems. The greater the depth or demands for accountability, the more testing and evaluation that is usually required. Statistical approaches can greatly assist the calculation of sample sizes, levels of confidence and other implications related to the cost of the audit and the coverage required to meet such demands. This advantage will become clearer during some of the case studies.

At a more operational management level, much depends on the general management style and ethos of your organization, but some of the advantages claimed for introducing statistical sampling include the following:

1   More accurate calculation of the optimal sample size for each test/test programme, (often reducing the size for larger accounts and audit assignments where previously sample size had been increased in simple proportion to population).
2   Agreement of parameters and audit coverage with client management strengthens any subsequent case for management action following unexpected error levels.
3   Planning and control of audits are generally enhanced by, for example:

  • setting clear objectives for testing;
  • clearly defining the nature of errors in relation to objectives;
  • deciding what rate or value of errors can be tolerated;
  • requiring a high standard of recording and reviewing of audit papers;
  • carefully considering the implications of each error discovered.

In fact a variety of improvements in audit management may arise from the introduction of statistical approaches, because they encourage a structured way of sampling which benefits many aspects of audit planning, testing and control. There is, of course, no reason in principle why the absence of statistical sampling should prevent any such benefits arising in the first place. But practical experience suggests that statistical sampling often introduces a challenge that focuses collective management efforts in this respect.

So far we have been keen to stress the advantages of statistical sampling but, to take full advantage, caution is required, particularly if, like many auditors, you have not introduced statistical approaches already.

Potential pitfalls and disadvantages

It is as well to be aware of these, as far as practical, before any widespread adoption of new sampling techniques.

The need for planning

We have already mentioned that statistical approaches can enhance audit planning, but it is vital to realize that, initially, these approaches must themselves be introduced on a planned basis. Perhaps there is no greater potential disadvantage than a botched attempt to force statistical sampling upon, hitherto, contented audit staff. Some time needs to be allowed for training audit staff, consulting audited client managers (particularly internal auditors) and introducing the sampling on a gradual basis. Some organizations have already done this, while others have 'tinkered' with statistical approaches sufficiently to be aware of the potential problems. Many larger external audit firms have, of course, already introduced statistical approaches as indicated in Table 1.1.

Cost of investing in new skills

This follows on from what we have just mentioned. The initial planning and eventual evaluation of findings will usually be the work of more experienced staff, though the actual audit tests themselves will, of course, not change as a result of the sampling approach. It is hoped that this book will offset at least some of the extra cost of training in new skills. An investment in new skills, while it involves an initial cost, will, like many other skills investments (in computer auditing, interviewing, and so on), pay back handsome dividends.

One of the drawbacks related to investment in new skills which, while it is unlikely to be widespread, can be particularly annoying to auditees is a tendency to use statistical techniques when non-statistical ones would have sufficed and been cheaper. One has to be careful that new skills do not incur such hidden costs as staff being trained at the client's expense, or wanting to use new skills simply because they have mastered them. This scenario is as bad as an accountant who uses his new computer to generate complex reports simply because it can, although no one else reads them.

An unrealistic sense of security

In some ways this point is similar to the comments made a little earlier on the issue of independence. The appearance of mathematical exactitude can lull the unwary into a false sense of security, particularly if statements are incomplete, or not completely understood by the readers of reports. Conclusions offering, say, a maximum error rate of 3.45 per cent relating to internal control events, or of £16 345 worth of monetary error in a balance of £145 million, need to be seen in terms of all the parameters of testing, including, in particular, confidence and risk. If, for example, these conclusions had been in terms of a 95 per cent confidence level (which is fairly common), then there would be a 5 per cent risk of being completely wrong. The same problem can sometimes arise with risk models where formulas give the impression of scientific accuracy when quite ordinary subjective judgments lie behind the weightings and calculations used. Clearly, auditors have a duty to ensure that the auditees appreciate the implications of their findings and to word these findings so that they can be quickly appreciated, if possible in 'jargon-free' language. We shall cover examples of this problem in the case studies.

Conclusion

Although the best professional standards encourage the use of statistical sampling, its main benefit to auditors lies in improving the value of their audits, particularly the audit testing of large transaction flows and balances.

Overall there are far more advantages than disadvantages to using statistical sampling provided that:

- it is introduced in a well-thought-out manner and preferably on a gradual basis;
- it does not become an end in itself, but is used strictly in the light of audit and testing objectives.

4 Theory, concepts and conditions

We have already touched upon some of these in our discussion so far and, although we mentioned at the start that this is not a book about statistics, most auditors will need to be aware of some of the fundamental points of theory and key sampling concepts. Such awareness will help you appreciate the wider context behind the main sampling approaches discussed in the following chapters. Indeed, many auditors will have covered the points raised in this chapter during their professional training and may wish to skip it altogether. But if you feel a little 'rusty' on these points or if you did not cover one or two of the concepts, such as the concept of a reliability factor, you may find this chapter useful.

Probability

This is basically a line of reasoning from common sense and practical observation. If you keep on tossing a coin, the probability is that you will end up with half the tosses as heads and half as tails, or if you keep on rolling a die, the chance or probability for each side tends to be a sixth, assuming of course the coins or dice are fair. Gamblers were among the early experts in probability, but nowadays probabilities can be obtained from tables or calculated by using computers, and they underpin much of the statistical theory upon which sampling relies.

The normal distribution

Jumping on a bit from the basic concept of probability, one of the most useful theories for statistical sampling is that of the 'normal' distribution. You may recall, if your accountancy or other previous training included statistics, the bell-shaped diagram used to describe this, which is shown below as Figure 4.1.

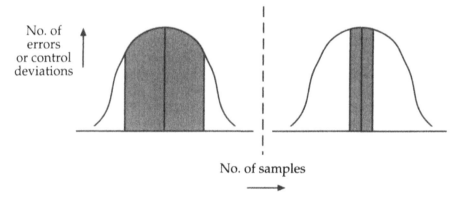

Figure 4.1   Normal distribution

In practice most accounting populations tend to be 'skewed' to the left, that is, they have more low-value transactions, though they may be almost any shape other than a perfect bell. But, if repeated, equally-sized samples are taken and then the number of errors or control deviations drawn on a graph, this will give the bell-shaped curve. This enables us to use the area under the bell-shaped curve to deduce the proportion or chance of samples having error occurrences within specified limits.

In the diagram the area under the bell-shaped curve represents the total number of samples. The number of samples having proportions of errors within any chosen range (acceptable limits) around the most common proportion of error (the middle line) is shown as shaded strips. The extent of the range determines the width of the strip.

Precision, confidence and point estimates

Any one sample picked for audit is more likely to be within an acceptable range, or acceptable limits, if the strip is wider. The auditor can set the width of the strip according to how accurate the results of the testing need to be, which is usually referred to as setting the 'precision' limits. Once the precision limits have been chosen, the probability that a particular audit sample will have an error value or rate within these limits is known and can be increased or decreased by varying the sample size. The auditor will be increasing or decreasing the risk and the 'confidence' that the sample result is a true representation of the population.

In practice these parameters are all interdependent and can usually be found from published tables, some of which we will use in the cases. Confidence is the complement of risk (i.e. 100 per cent minus risk) thus an acceptable risk of 5 per cent implies 95 per cent confidence. The level of precision, confidence and sample size must be balanced against each other to suit the auditor's judgment of the level of assurance required from the audit testing. At the back of the auditor's mind will be the level of risk that can be tolerated from not testing all the items – the higher the level of acceptable risk, the lower the level of confidence, and, within any particular precision limits, the smaller the sample size.

Let us look again at the three vital ingredients, p. 10, of a typical conclusion from statistical sampling. In terms of the foregoing discussion these can be stated as:

1   *a point estimate*, that is, the best estimate of the population characteristic based on our extrapolation from sample results, usually in auditing the value of errors in a balance or the rate of control deviations in a system;

2   *our confidence that the sample results are correct*, that is, the complement of risk of sampling error (note: 'sampling error' is based on the risk that a correctly evaluated sample will still not be a correct reflection of the population – the unavoidable risk that comes from not testing all items. Sampling error should not be confused with 'non-sampling error' that comes from a variety of possibilities of human error, such as an incorrect reading or an inaccurate transcription of results);

3   *our chosen precision levels*, this can be expressed in terms of an upper, or a lower, precision level, or the range between an upper and a lower level. In practice auditors tend to be more concerned with the upper (or maximum) precision level for errors.

Typical examples of conclusions from audit testing might be:

From our sampling results the best estimate of total monetary error in the payroll for the year (the population) is £1 240 (the point estimate) and we are 95 per cent confident (confidence level) that the true value of error in the population lies between £1 000 and £1 500 (the precision range).

From our sample we estimate internal control to be ineffective in 3.5 per cent of control events and we are 90 per cent confident that the true rate in the population of events is between 3 per cent and 5 per cent.

As already mentioned, in practice auditors tend to be more concerned with upper precision limits, that is, the maximum tolerable error rates or the upper error level resulting from the extrapolation, as these are the 'worst-case situations' and that is more usually in line with a prudent approach to reporting. Thus a conclusion might be summarized as:

We are 95 per cent confident that the (maximum) upper error level is no greater than £12 100, in the balance of £10 million.

We are 95 per cent confident that the (maximum) deviation rate of internal control was 3 per cent or less over the time that control was in operation.

The reliability factor

We said that various tables are available to the auditor, but perhaps one of the most useful tables in practice is Table 4.1 below. (It can be derived from cumulative poisson probabilities which appear in many standard sets of mathematical tables. The numbers of sample errors are assumed to be the random events and the reliability factors are in fact the average number of events per interval.) For convenience and to minimize the number of tables the auditor needs to consult during a typical audit, Table 4.1 is ideal and has gained popularity. More extensive versions can be found in CIPFA's guide *Statistics for Audit* (see Appendix 6). (If you want to calculate your own version, look up the cumulative poisson probabilities table in Appendix 5. The average

Table 4.1   Reliability factors*

No. of sample errors	Required confidence level %						
	70	75	80	85	90	95	99
0	1.21	1.39	1.61	1.90	2.31	3.00	4.61
1	2.44	2.69	3.00	3.38	3.89	4.75	6.64
2	3.62	3.92	4.28	4.73	5.33	6.30	8.41
3	4.77	5.11	5.52	6.02	6.69	7.76	10.05
4	5.90	6.28	6.73	7.27	8.00	9.16	11.61

*From cumulative poisson probabilities.

The reliability factor is a convenient mechanism for determining the sample size in terms of the required confidence level and the anticipated level of errors. Other things being equal the more confidence required the larger the sample, similarly the more frequent or greater the value of errors the larger the sample.

number of events per interval (*m*) corresponds to the reliability factor, the probability of *r* or more random events to the number of errors +1, and the confidence levels to the probabilities in the table.)

This table assumes the auditor will make a judgment about the level of risk and, thus, the confidence required for testing and also about the likelihood of errors actually occurring in the sample. Using these, a reliability factor can be read from the table and used in several standard formulas which we shall consider in the next chapter.

Underlying this table is an assumption that the poisson distribution, which is different from the normal distribution, is a reliable working approximation. Also, for most sampling situations the practical assumption is that not many errors are likely to exist in the population or be picked up in the sample. If either of these assumptions is invalid, perhaps because populations are small or error rates large (usually over 10 per cent), auditors are advised to seek expert advice, though it is generally considered that, if the auditor knows that error rates are high and large numbers are likely to be picked up from the sample, there is little point in sampling in the first place, as an unacceptable conclusion has already been reached judgmentally.

The population

This is a term we have already used but without defining it (see Appendix 2 for a glossary of terms). The population, a simple concept in theory, is a vital concept to get right in practice as soon as sampling is planned. For statistical sampling purposes it must be large (usually over 1 000, though less may be acceptable) and made up of the same things, that is, it must be homogeneous. For example, debtors' and creditors' transactions will usually be separate populations, as will stocks and salaries. Separate stores or payrolls might be considered separate populations, but this would depend on the systems involved and objectives, for example, whether the auditor is forming an opinion on year-end figures for the whole organization or undertaking several different assignments. Likewise, salaries and wages may be treated as two separate populations or a single one, depending on the audit objectives. Professional judgment on the part of the person planning the audit is critical when defining the boundaries of the population.

The population characteristic

This is basically the property we wish to investigate and about which we will form a statistical conclusion. Typical characteristics will be the rate of internal control deviations or the value of errors. For these purposes most of our time will be spent considering attribute sampling and monetary unit sampling, the reasons for which will become clear in the next few chapters. Where the characteristic relates to estimates of variables such as population means or standard deviations, variable sampling is more appropriate.

Sampling units

Again, something that is often taken for granted at a theoretical level may need more careful consideration in practice. If one of the controls to be sampled during an audit is the signed authorization of weekly time sheets, then individual time sheets will be the sampling units, for example, rather than say the weekly wages printouts. Similarly, in monetary unit sampling, (see Chapter 7) individual pounds, dollars, and so on will be the sampling units, rather than invoices, orders or other financial records.

Access to the sample (sampling frames)

Clearly, it is pointless to plan a sample and then find that the sampling units cannot actually be accessed or their completeness guaranteed. The sampling frame is simply the physical listing or method that gives access to the sample. Ideally, this will coincide with the population, but at times it may be a more practically accessible or a complete, surrogate. For example, payroll leavers may be sampled from personnel records rather than the payroll, and a sample of council tax payers from a property register.

Errors

An audited population may reveal a wide range of possible error types: deviations in various internal controls; amounts that are *ultra vires*; simple arithmetic miscalculations; and so on. Each type of error will relate to one or more characteristics of the population, such as monetary values, regulatory requirements, authorizations, reconciliations, and so on. Different types of error will often relate to different audit objectives and to different tests. The auditor must be clear about what types of error will relate to the particular objectives of each audit and each test or test programme.

On a non-statistical basis it may be acceptable to simply list a wide range of errors with little or no attempt to prioritize, though even then it is not the best practice. In a statistical context it is particularly important to be clear about what constitutes an error in relation to the objectives and the population over which the errors are to be extrapolated.

If, for example, one is testing for over- or underpayment, the fact that a payment may have been irregularly authorized, or coded to lighting rather than heating, will not usually affect the conclusion about the value of over- or underpayments in the population. Of course, management will need to be informed about such incidental errors that come to light and there may be important ramifications, but if such errors were included in one's sampling extrapolation or conclusion, this would give an incorrect result. Similarly, if an audit objective relates to the application of certain internal controls in a system, any errors the controls were not designed to prevent should not be included in the statistical evaluation. Perhaps minor distance measurements on travel and subsistence claims, though errors would not be covered by a senior manager's authorization, or perhaps purchases of poor value would not count as errors among invoices tested for authorization by a budget holder.

Random (or known chance) selection

We have already considered this concept, but it is a vital concept to maintain throughout your statistical sampling. Clearly, random selection, because it ensures that each item in the population has an equal chance of selection, so avoiding bias, is the generally applicable approach. Confusion sometimes arises over probability-proportional-to-size approaches such as monetary unit sampling because, the higher the recorded value of the transactions, the more chance they have of being selected. But here it is each pound or other monetary unit that has an equal chance of being selected and which enables us to draw monetary conclusions, which is the point of the exercise. It also makes extrapolation of errors a little more complicated, but more on this later.

Conclusion

Although this is not a book about statistics, some key concepts have been outlined for the sake of presenting as complete as practical a picture in the context of audit sampling.

Perhaps more important than the fine details of theory is an awareness of the underlying concepts, such as probability, and the practical implications of statistical concepts, such as the population.

If you find any of these concepts a little difficult at this stage, return to this chapter after you have followed through some of the examples and case studies. People often take a while to become familiar with the use of reliability factors on first encountering tables such as Table 4.1.

5   Attribute sampling

We have already mentioned this as one of the main approaches that auditors are likely to find useful. Basically, attribute sampling measures the presence or absence of a particular population characteristic, or attribute, each time a sample unit is tested. This is a 'yes/no' situation: either the attribute is present, or it is not.

There are different types of attribute sampling and we cannot realistically cover each one fully during a work of reasonable length for auditors who need a practical introduction. The most straightforward and widely applicable in a practical context is called 'the poisson approximation to the binomial' and is particularly appropriate when error rates are low, as described on p. 34 when outlining the reliability factor. Sample sizes may be slightly larger than with other techniques, but ease of application is generally considered to outweigh this small disadvantage.

The yes/no situation mentioned above is one which applies to most compliance testing of internal controls. It is, therefore, in tests of internal controls that attribute sampling comes into its own. Generally speaking, either a control has operated or it has not. A few 'grey areas' may very occasionally come to light

– perhaps the recognition of a signature or the reality of separation between duties – but these are almost invariably due to some inadequacy in the manner of evidencing the control operation rather than in the control concept itself. Provided the auditor is satisfied that adequate evidence of the operation of internal control is present, this is a 'yes', otherwise, whatever the reason, it is a 'no'.

In practice these are usually fairly simple and undisputed characteristics, such as signed authorizations, password security, official stamps, recorded evidence of who did what, and so on.

Attribute sample size

Complex statistical calculations such as standard deviations or precise knowledge of population size are not usually required to work out a sample size for which the following is the most commonly used formula:

Sample size = reliability factor / precision proportion

In this case, as long as the precision is expressed as a proportion, usually the percentage maximum tolerable error rate (the upper precision level), the sample size will be the same for any large population.

Sampling interval

Clearly, the sample could be picked by using a simple random selection perhaps from random number tables (see Appendix 5). Or, if the items are recorded on computerized systems, as is nearly always the case nowadays, either a random sample can be generated using available reporting facilities, or the data can be downloaded to the auditor's computer and randomly sampled using a range of audit software currently available.

In manually-held records the auditor is generally advised to use interval sampling already mentioned above on p. 13. The following formula is convenient, though the auditor needs to ensure that the population is numbered consecutively before sampling from random number tables, as explained in Appendix 5.

Fixed sampling interval
= Number of items in population / Sample size

Let's consider a simple case.

Case study 1: compliance testing during a stock system audit

During the audit of a stock control system Rhianon the auditor identifies the signing of stores issues notes by authorized budget holders as one of the key internal controls. Evidence of past audits is available, she has visited the stores, examined the current procedures and has reviewed the systems documentation and control.

Rhianon and the stores manager both agree that very few errors occur in the operation of this particular key control. Of 12 000 issue notes received during the past year the manager can only recall a few being sent back because they were not properly signed. After considering the role of this control in the wider system and the results of previous years' audits it is felt that compliance testing of this control must be sufficient to give assurance that the maximum error rate in the population (of control operations over the year) is no more than 4 per cent. Rhianon wants to be 90 per cent confident of her results and does not anticipate finding any errors in the sample.

Consider:

- the sample size;
- the sampling interval;

- what to conclude if no errors are found;
- what to conclude if one or more errors are found.

Suggestions

Using the formula above, p. 40 it is probably best to consider this scenario in two stages:

1   First find the reliability factor from Table 4.1.
2   Fit the factor into the formula to find the sample size.

This is summarized below.

Step 1

Looking across the top of Table 4.1, we come to a '90 per cent confidence' level, which is the confidence the auditor has judged appropriate for her testing. The next judgment we need is the auditor's assumption of errors that will be found in the sample: none are expected. The intersection of the '90 per cent confidence' column and the row for '0 errors' gives a reliability factor of 2.31.

Step 2

The reliability factor of 2.31 is divided by the maximum tolerable error rate (MTER) the auditor (and the manager?) feel could be allowed for this type of internal control, that is, 4 per cent.

$$2.31 / 0.04 = 57.75$$

We will call this 58 items (it is always necessary to round up, as one can not test part of an internal control!).

In practice, then, the auditor would now choose a random sample of 58 stores issues notes to test. (No doubt several internal controls would be examined in a typical stock control system and, providing the same parameters are applied to all, the same sample size would arise. It is often the case that only one or a very small number of key documents need to be sampled, regardless of whether a statistical or non-statistical approach is adopted.)

If this was to be done manually, a sampling interval would need to be calculated using the formula given above.

Sampling interval = population / sample size

$$\frac{\text{Population}}{\text{sample size}} \quad \frac{12\,000}{58} = 206.9$$

This time, because we cannot measure 0.9 of an item for testing, we will round down rather than up, so as to be on the safe side. As explained in Appendix 5, a random start point between 1 and 206 will be picked and 206 added to this every interval. If the random start was 80 then (adding 206 each time) the
80th,
286th,
492nd,
and so on,
item would be extracted, up to the
11 822nd

The actual serial number of each item extracted would depend in this case on the sequential numbers of the year's stores issue sheets.

If no errors are found: the auditor can conclude that the system control seems to have operated to the standards expected, that is, she is 90 per cent confident that the true error rate in the population is less than 4 per cent.

If an error is found: the simplest conclusion is that the control does not seem to have operated to the standards required, that is, one cannot be 90 per cent confident that the true error rate in the population is less than 4 per cent.

It is important to consider how you will put your conclusions to management, since it is easy to give a wrong impression. Perhaps because no errors were found in the sample, the auditor is saying that he or she is confident none exist in the population.

In this example, if an error were found, the auditor might

decide to recalculate the sample size allowing for one error. This would give a reliability factor of 3.89 and a sample size of

$$3.89 / 0.04 = 97.25 \text{ (say 98)}$$

In the table we have used the auditor would need to re-sample. Tables for situations where the auditor wishes to pick a sample and possibly extend it, if more errors than initially assumed are found, are based on sampling with replacement (see, for example, in *Statistics for Audit* by CIPFA, Table 3.3, p. 102). However, most audit situations assume sampling without replacement. Such tables give larger sample sizes and readers are advised to be cautious and perhaps seek statistical advice before using them. Many auditors would ask: if the initial parameters were the right ones for a particular audit, why change them just because the system is not as good as at first thought? This is perhaps the time to involve managers in further testing and/or system improvement.

If one had looked, for example, for a reliability factor of 2.31, assuming one error from sampling, the associated confidence level in Table 4.1 would have been below 70 per cent and, therefore, not included (it would have been about 66 per cent). At the planning stage of sampling would anyone have suggested that an auditor who tests to a 90 per cent confidence level should consider a 66 per cent level?

Clearly, too, if several control deviations were found, the position regarding this particular internal control would become unacceptable to any reasonable auditor.

From Case Study 5 the following key decisions emerge upon which the auditor must bring professional judgment to bear:

- *The required confidence level.* It is likely in practice that this will be common to most testing, perhaps the most popular confidence levels for audit testing are 90 per cent or 95 per cent.
- *The anticipated number of sample errors.* This type of attribute sampling tends to be fairly intolerant of sample errors, and

it is not suggested that more than one or two errors are allowed for. In fact, the best policy is probably to introduce attribute sampling on reliable systems and allow for nil errors.

● *The maximum tolerable error rate in the population.* This is not to be confused with any estimated actual error rate, perhaps from past audit findings, or management quality control procedures, or control risk self-assessment testing. The system may well be thought to have an internal control error rate lower than the auditor or managers would accept for audit purposes.

From this the sample size is simply reliability factor/MTER and the sampling interval is simply population/sample size. The rest of the audit testing proceeds as usual. In fact, modern audit software can simply present the sample on screen once the auditor has keyed in the chosen parameters. By introducing these relatively minor statistical steps into their sampling, however, auditors can reap considerable benefits in terms of much more useful and measurable conclusions.

The formula used above may be rearranged if it suits the situation. Sometimes it is more convenient to see what parameters can be achieved for any given sample size, particularly what level of precision, or MTER.

MTER = reliability factor / sample size

For, say, 95 per cent confidence level and no sample errors expected – that is, a reliability factor of 3.0 – an auditor wishing to sample only 30 items could expect to offer assurance that the MTER in the population was no more than 10 per cent (3 / 30), subject of course to finding no errors and the 5 per cent sampling risk implied in the 95 per cent confidence level. An auditor prepared to test 150 items to the same parameters could expect to offer assurance that MTER was no more than 2 per cent, and so on.

Depending on your particular approach to auditing and the standards expected, you can build up your own tables in terms of sample sizes, confidence levels or whatever you consider the vital parameters of your audit planning. Alternatively, you may find it more convenient to rework the formulas for each assignment, as the effort is not excessive compared to the time spent on most main audit assignments. Table 9.2, p. 110, gives an example.

Let us consider another case study and some of the wider implications of using attribute sampling during compliance testing.

Case study 2: compliance testing a purchases system

Bill is planning to audit a purchases system and has identified three key controls for all central purchases:

1   The authorization of the purchase orders by a limited number of budget-holder managers.
2   The separation between budget holders and the central purchasing officer who also signs each order to confirm compliance with purchasing policy, including obtaining quotes and tenders as appropriate.
3   The exclusive use of official, sequentially-prenumbered purchase orders, (top copy to the supplier, undercopies to budget holders and purchasing officer).

He wishes to be 95 per cent confident of any conclusions arrived at from testing. At this organization the first two key controls are expected to operate effectively 98 per cent of the time, that is, with a MTER of 2 per cent. However, after discussions with the managers it is found that the third key control is always expected to operate effectively, that is, with an MTER of nil.

Bill's past experience leads him to allow for nil compliance errors when testing the first control, and one when testing the second.

Consider:

- the sample sizes calculated from the formula;
- what sample sizes will actually be tested;
- the implications if

   a) no errors are found,
   b) one error is found related to the second key control,
   c) one or more errors relating to the first and third key controls,
   d) any other combination of errors.

How much assurance could Bill offer this organization if he was restricted to testing a maximum of 100 items?

Suggestions

From Table 4.1 the reliability factor for nil errors and 95 per cent confidence is 3.0. If one sample error is allowed for, the reliability factor increases to 4.75.

For the first control the sample size from the formula, p. 40 is

$$3.00 / 0.02 = 150$$

and for the second control

$$4.75 / 0.02 = 237.5 \text{ (say 238)}$$

As both the above controls in this case are evidenced on the same sheets of paper, then clearly, if one has to look at 238 orders for the signature of the central purchasing officer, one might as well look at the signature of the authorizing manager as well.

If each control was evidenced on separate sheets, two separate samples would be extracted – one of 150 and one of 238, and if, for some reason, the manager's signatures took a long time to verify, two separate samples might be worthwhile.

With regard to the requirement for nil MTER on the third control, this level of perfection means that one would, strictly, have to examine all control events in the chosen population. Since it is often impractical for the auditor to check every one of a large number of control events, it is often desirable to ask management to agree to a low level of MTER, simply for testing purposes.

If, perhaps, in this case, the auditor had to count manually through a large series of orders to reach the items to be sampled on an interval basis, this might well give complete assurance of their sequential numbering. Similarly, if the records were held on computer, it might well be possible to check the sequential numbering using available report-generation facilities or by downloading to the auditor's computer. If indeed this control were vital, the auditor might well ask why no software check was written into the program to ensure that the order number was generated sequentially each time an order was produced.

If no errors, or only one, error relating to the second key control had been found, then the chosen parameters would have held and the auditor could offer assurance about the purchasing system along the lines of

operating to within agreed standards

95 per cent confident that the MTER in the population of control operations relating to the purchasing system is no greater than 2 per cent

or whatever is judged most suitable for a particular organization.

If only one error more than planned for had been found relating to the first two controls, we would then have a situation similar to the last case study. One could perhaps re-sample or rearrange the parameters. Once a more frequent combination of errors is found, however, the auditor is unlikely to find the controls operating to a satisfactory level, however the parameters are viewed. Clearly in this case even one error relating to the third control would lead to a conclusion that this was unacceptable.

If the auditor is constrained to select a sample of only 100 then, assuming the same confidence level and anticipated error rate is used, this will offer 95 per cent confidence that the MTER is no more than:

reliability factor / sample size = 3 / 100 = 3%

For some auditors this sort of analysis provides a convenient link between the level of testing that the audited client managers are prepared to pay for and the value of the work, in terms of level of assurance, that they can expect. This can be particularly useful in an internal audit situation where senior managers are sometimes reluctant to fund audit testing, since they see it as the most expensive element of the audit, though this often turns out not to be the case, particularly if internal audit is subsequently called in to report on why a system 'failed'. Perhaps one of the most valuable uses of attribute sampling for compliance testing comes in offering assurance to audit committees and to board members in general.

Since the advent of the 'Cadbury' report in the UK and the 'COSO' report in the USA (see Appendix 6 entries for both reports) more and more organizations have adopted such committees. Most annual reports of listed plcs contain a statement regarding the board's opinion of the soundness of internal control in their company. Most of the evidence for such opinions comes via audit reports to the board, and the bulk of the findings relate to the testing of internal control in the main financial systems. Gone are the 'easy' days when the auditor could simply review control arrangements, that is, ask a few reasonably predictable questions. Committees want assurance that will stand up to scrutiny and is in line with the best professional standards.

Conclusion

Attribute sampling basically considers a yes/no situation ideally suited to compliance testing of internal control. The auditor's skill and judgment are mostly called for in planning the sample and interpreting the results. Care is also required in deciding how the conclusions are to be reported to management. It is important not to use jargon when common terms would suffice, and to report in a style that suits the particular managers who will read the report.

Once the sampling has been set up and the auditor has gained familiarity with the techniques, it is unlikely that much more time will be added to significant assignments covering the main financial systems of large organizations. The potential value of attribute sampling will far outstrip likely costs.

6 An introduction to monetary unit sampling (MUS)

Attribute sampling, as discussed in the previous chapter, is fine as a test of internal control, since the items being sampled, control events, have no monetary value in themselves. However, as soon as auditors or their clients ask about the financial implications of testing, particularly of error levels, something further is needed. Monetary unit sampling has largely replaced other (variables sampling and non-statistical) methods in terms of its effectiveness in offering assurance regarding the value of errors in the account balances; in essence, the reliability in terms of the accuracy of the system output.

MUS has been developed by external rather than internal auditors, mainly for use in substantive rather than compliance testing. But it is fair to say that internal auditors are finding it increasingly useful.

Substantive or compliance testing and the role of MUS

It is worth pausing a while to consider the roles of compliance and substantive testing. Both are widely used in internal and

51

external audit work. As in recent years the internal audit role has become increasingly concerned with the security and control of main financial systems, internal auditors (particularly in relatively small units set up in response to Cadbury) have had to place increasing reliance on compliance testing of internal control as part of their systems-based audit (SBA). As many internal auditors realize, however, in the long run the most reliable evidence that the internal controls are operating effectively is the reliability of the system output, and its accuracy and validity. The only direct evidence of the reliability of system output is substantive, checking the completeness, accuracy and validity of records against supporting documents, trends, events and observation.

Substantive testing is, however, usually much more expensive than compliance testing. Most records, vouchers and other direct evidence have to be examined in detail, recalculated, reperformed and so on, as distinct from simply looking for signatures, key entries in computer-recorded fields, official stamps, and the like. This has always been one of the arguments in favour of directing effort to systems evaluation and compliance testing: provided one can rely on the evidence of control operation, indirect though it may be, it is far more economic and efficient to gather. The sheer size of modern systems precludes testing the very large samples of transactions upon which direct substantive testing (DST) alone traditionally relied.

However, in recent years some auditors have been surprised to discover that samples taken using MUS have been smaller and more efficient than they might have expected. To be frank, others have also been surprised to find that the smaller substantive test sample sizes, already used on a non-statistical basis, would offer so little measurable assurance as to be virtually a waste of time. The advantages of calculating an optimal sample size for each particular audit can bring efficiency and effectiveness to bear in what in the past has often been a hit-or-miss approach.

Most auditors, particularly internal ones, would be reluctant to view DST simply as an alternative to SBA. For one thing,

SBA is seen as a means of ensuring that the system controls are able to guard against future risks, whereas DST tends to look back at past system output and performance. However, within SBA most auditors would supplement compliance testing with substantive testing depending on the reliability of the internal controls in each system, often deciding on the sample size as control failures are identified. Increasingly nowadays, internal auditors are using MUS to add value to their substantive testing as part of their routine systems testing of main financial systems. At the same time, external auditors are increasingly seeing MUS as a more efficient short cut to forming opinions on large account balances.

As we shall see in the case studies, it is not always necessary to take different samples for compliance and substantive testing using MUS, and this further increases the potential room for cooperation between internal and external auditors.

Some of the issues discussed in this section in relation to risk are discussed further in Chapter 8 under Risk Models.

The purpose and pitfalls of MUS

From what we said at the start of this chapter it should be clear that MUS is used to offer a conclusion in money terms about the accuracy of account balances. In fact, the probability-proportional-to-size sampling approach, of which MUS is the best-known example for auditors, is basically used to offer assurance about whatever output the system records. In auditing the main financial systems this will be account balances over a period of time, but in non-financial systems it could be assurance about weights recorded, the quality of product in terms of measured composition, and so on.

Because of the current importance of financial systems and records, we will stick to monetary rather than non-monetary units. But it is worth appreciating that wider possibilities exist for management audit in general.

Sample size and sampling interval for MUS

Conveniently, we can use a formula for calculating sample size similar to that used earlier for compliance testing with attribute sampling.

Sample size = (£ population × reliability factor) / £ precision

This effectively takes account of monetary values, rather than straightforward percentages as earlier.
The sampling interval is:

Sampling interval = £ population / sample size

The population is, as we said, the account balance or other value of the system output. The precision in the denominator of the equation for sample size is, in effect, the total value of errors that the auditor feels can be tolerated in the population; it is the upper end of the precision range as discussed on p. 32. Precision is, in fact, often taken to be synonymous with materiality, which in a narrow financial sense is understandable, though for many organizations the auditor's value for materiality is rather subjectively arrived at after taking account of the wider sensitivity and other non-financial implications of particular balances. Other terms used for the precision include 'upper error limit' (UEL) and 'maximum tolerable error level' (MTEL). In practice, a lower-than-maximum-tolerable amount may be used to calculate a slightly larger sample size to allow for some value of errors. This latter practice will be considered in the next chapter when we look at some of the more complicated aspects of MUS.

When using MUS, each single pound making up a balance is a sampling unit. (Perhaps it would be more appropriate to call this technique pound unit sampling or PUS!) Each pound selected for the sample is used to 'pull out' the transaction of which it is a part, and it is the transaction that is actually tested, just as it would be if it were chosen on a non-statistical basis.

Thus, the more pounds there are in any particular transaction, the more chance it has of being selected, that is, the probability is proportional to its size (PPS).

The mechanics of selection usually involve either a manual or computerized 'adding through' the population to reach the selected pounds (Case Study 3 shows this) and it is important to ensure that one recommences adding from the next pound after the one selected, not from the next pound after the transaction tested.

This PPS characteristic means that MUS tends to 'favour' overstatement errors. Overstatements increase the size of a transaction and the probability of its being selected; understatements decrease the size of a transaction, reducing the probability of its selection. Of course, any transactions recorded as 'nil value' will not be selected at all using MUS.

Some initial precautions

Because of these characteristics the following considerations are suggested at the planning stage of any audit for which MUS is likely:

- Take out any nil balances if it is planned to test these, and test them on a separate basis.
- Interval and cell selection: for convenience take out any large items that are bound to be selected because they are greater than the sampling interval. (It does not really matter if you leave them in: you will simply select from a larger population and might happen to hit them twice, while only testing them once, of course.)

Most systems process net transactions, and so total debit balances contain some credit entries and vice versa. Most audits will be equally concerned for an under- or overpayment, however it may be caused and even if errors offset one another, rather than just the net accuracy of the transaction. Thus, for example, it is a good idea to reverse the entries of any refunds or credit notes in a payment system, or gross up all the adjustments on transaction flows, so that each pound in the system, whether it acts as a debit or credit, has an equal chance of being selected. This is not usually difficult in practice.

Computerized transaction-processing systems usually display gross amounts and the totals of debits and credits in a form convenient for sampling. Even in manual systems a trial balance at a convenient point will give the totals to be added to find the monetary population. Sometimes the counter-entries may be so infrequent and immaterial as to be easily recognized and either ignored or examined manually. Examples of this may be: entries that are always made gross; possibly receipts at a rent office; or some types of refunds may not allow for netting off. Any opposite entries in such circumstances will usually be for the correction of clerical errors and easily recognizable.

On a judgmental basis exclude any known risky or unusual items and test these separately, as for nil balances. These are sometimes called 'key items'. This should leave the vast bulk of the population to be sampled on an MUS basis. Ideally, it should be a population for which few errors are actually thought to exist. As with attribute sampling, MUS is rather intolerant of errors, and when several are extrapolated to the population they usually result in breaching any reasonable parameters chosen.

Apart from these planning considerations the key decisions that the auditor must make at the start of MUS are similar to those noted for attribute sampling:

- The required confidence level.
- Anticipated number of sample errors, usually nil.
  (These two decisions enable the reliability factor to be obtained, see Table 4.1.)
- The precision (UEL, MTEL).

Let's consider a basic case study where the auditor makes no particular allowance for finding monetary errors.

Case study 3: external audit of year-end creditor's figure

An external auditor is substantively testing a year-end sundry creditor's balance recorded as £2 470 890. Materiality for the whole accounts under audit has been set at £540 000. The auditor wishes to be 90 per cent confident of the testing results. A brief examination of the year-end creditor's listing shows 7 000 credits totalling £2 470 990 and three debits totalling £100, netting to the recorded balance. There is a very similar pattern to previous years and the auditor concludes that no sample errors are anticipated.

The individual amounts listed are mainly very small in comparison to the balance being audited, though one particularly large payment of £224 900 stands out. There are also two items listed as nil balances, which also stand out in the listing and are in any case listed separately at the end of the printout.

Consider:

- the basic precision;
- key items;
- the population to be sampled;
- the sample size;
- how the sample might be extracted;
- what to conclude if no errors are found;
- what to do if errors are found from testing.

Suggestions

In this case we are left to assume that the auditor will simply take the materiality for the accounts (or an agreed proportion) as the basic precision. This will minimize the cost of testing, provided the auditor is correct in these assumptions. It is often assumed that, as an external auditor, one should minimize the cost of expensive substantive testing by seeking no more than reasonable assurance that a material error is not present as each balance is tested. In this case the auditor considers 90 per cent confidence as reasonable.

Before sampling, the auditor extracts from the year-end list totalling £2 471 090 (£2 470 990 + £100) the nil items and the one very large item of £224 900 to test separately. His conclusions on these will be taken into account, together with the results of his sample testing, to form a conclusion about the possibility of material error on this balance.

The auditor should take the total gross credit and debit pounds as the population, though in this case (as often happens) the netting-off items are so small as to make no significant difference. Strictly speaking, the final population to be sampled will be £2 246 190, (compared to the recorded balance after taking out key items of £2 245 990).

The sample size will be (population × reliability factor / precision):

$$£2\ 246\ 190 \times 2.31 / £540\ 000 = 9.6\ (\text{i.e. }10)\ \text{items}$$

The sampling interval will be:

$$£2\ 246\ 190 / 10 = \text{every }£224\ 619\text{th pound}$$

The sample items, if selected by computer, might be extracted from a simple random sample of ten single pounds out of the whole population, each pound 'hit' pulling out to be tested the transaction of which it forms a part.

More usually, perhaps, a random selection of one item per 'cell' might be made from ten cells, each one sampling interval wide.

It is conceivable that for a well-documented listing of this size the auditor might decide to simply add, manually, through the list, selecting each £224 619th pound after selecting a random start from between 1 and 224 618. Again, each pound selected would pull out a transaction to test.

It is worth recalling at this point that, manually, the pounds in the three debit items should each be included as a credit and part of the transaction to which it relates. (If say, a transaction was made up of a year-end credit of £78 due to a supplier, plus a debit of £20 relating to a credit note from that supplier, giving a net recorded value of £58, it would be counted as £98 as the population is added through and sampled.)

If no errors are found either from the sample or the key items, as with the attribute sampling cases, one could simply say

the parameters have held

the balance appears to be correctly stated within the limits of the parameters chosen

the audit testing indicates errors in the year-end creditor's balance are unlikely to amount to a material level

[in more quantified terms] the testing indicates we can be 90 per cent confident errors in the year-end creditor's are less than £540 000

or, whatever wording fits your organization's reporting style and client requirements.

If errors are found, the auditor's most obvious conclusion is simply that the risk of a material error being present in the year-end creditor's is unacceptable. Clearly, however this is actually worded, most circumstances would require some further testing or other audit work, or possibly testing by management. The approach so far has been very similar to the cases involving attribute sampling in the previous chapter.

However, in practice most auditors would try some form of extrapolation to form an opinion about the new upper error level, that is, the level of precision that could be associated with the errors found. This raises the question of how to extrapolate errors found during MUS, which we shall consider in the next chapter.

Case study 4: the internal audit of a creditor's payment system

Let us assume that an internal auditor is auditing the creditor's payments system that gave rise to the year-end figures in the last case.

The population throughput for the year, since the last audit, has been £24 080 000. The internal auditor too expects few errors in the population and none in any sample. The system controls have been compliance-tested and found to operate soundly within the parameters chosen, but the internal auditor never relies solely on this indirect evidence for main financial systems, preferring to obtain some direct substantive evidence.

Consider:

- the level of precision that should be used for internal audit testing;
- the confidence level you would select;
- any other influences that might be appropriate to choosing parameters in internal auditing;
- the sample size you get from the above considerations;
- the effect that the internal auditor's role may have on the population used for testing.

Suggestions

In an internal audit scenario (and some external ones) the simple decision to accept materiality for the accounts as a whole as precision for testing each balance is often thought inappropriate: the auditor is not trying to form an opinion on the accuracy of the accounts as a whole. Each individual system may require a separate reassessment of precision (MTEL, UEL) for testing purposes.

It is therefore unlikely that, on a system-by-system basis, the large level of materiality acceptable to an external auditor would be equally acceptable to an internal auditor. On a system-by-system basis the materiality could well be lower than the external auditor, while at the same time some populations of transaction values may be higher. 'Creditor's throughput' for the year, for example, would be a much higher value than 'year-end creditor's', whereas, by contrast, fixed-asset accounting systems usually process a lower value of purchases, sale, and revaluations than the total value of assets at the year end.

In general the lower (that is, more demanding) precision levels used in internal auditing, particularly when, as in this case, they are combined with larger populations, give much larger sample sizes than in the last case. To some extent this follows expected practice where internal auditors tend to take larger samples than external auditors when undertaking audit testing.

It is, however, often true that, as the internal auditor will have built up a wealth of evidence about a system from reviewing and evaluating the internal controls in some detail, they will seek a lower level of confidence, that is, they will accept a higher level of risk than would be the case in the basic external audit scenario considered in the last case. (The same consideration may apply to external auditors if they have the same level of systems evidence available.)

In addition to these simple monetary values and percentages an internal auditor, and some external auditors, may decide to take other factors into consideration, such as the sensitivity of particular systems – for example, bonus payments, directors' emoluments, councillors' expenses, and so on.

The internal auditor would probably seek to consult the relevant managers before coming to a conclusion about precision. The same consultation may well apply to the consideration of confidence level.

In Chapter 3 we discussed the advantage of using statistical sampling to bring managers into the decision-making at the audit-planning stage. The internal auditor would normally already have in mind some minimal level of testing and assurance in terms of confidence and precision. Nevertheless, managers can often shed light on the population by helping to identify key items. Their concern in terms of the level of error resulting from human fallibility that they would 'tolerate' is often a useful factor in choosing precision.

Thus, the precision and confidence levels used by an internal auditor are generally likely to vary far more than those used by an external auditor at the same organization.

In this case the population of a year's worth of creditor payments comes to £20 080 000 and, for the sake of illustration, let us assume that managers and auditors are happy to choose a confidence level of 75 per cent and precision of £200 000. This would give a sample size of:

$$£20\,080\,000 \times 1.39 \,/\, 200\,000 = 139.56 \text{ (say 140)}$$

In practice this is quite a large sample to test all at once. A single auditor would, perhaps, take a week or more depending on the complexity of documentation and the arrangements in place. It will often be more convenient to test intermittently at convenient points in time throughout the year rather than tie up staff for a long period.

In the face of relatively large sample sizes it is becoming increasingly common to adopt a stance more akin to external audit and seek to agree an overall precision or materiality for the organization as a whole, or at least for the financial systems as a whole, rather like the external audit materiality for the accounts as a whole. This is perhaps best agreed at director/audit committee level, and may involve some adjustment to the materiality used by external audit, or may well be based on budgeted figures for the coming year rather than past historical accounts figures. This latter approach is considered more in line with the internal auditor's role in examining what *is* happening rather than what *has* happened in an organization.

If the internal auditor in this case took a materiality level more in line with the external auditor's accounts, materiality in the last case this might be, say, £500 000, giving a sample size using the above parameters, of:

$$£20\,080\,000 \times 1.39 \,/\, £500\,000 = 55.8 \text{ (say 56)}$$

By taking account of risk and materiality in a structured manner in line with board and/or audit committee agreement, the

auditor has gradually reduced the sample size to a more efficient, but still justifiable, level. We shall see in Chapter 8 that it
is possible to use risk models to take account of the reduced
level of risk associated with obtaining assurance/confidence
from audit findings other than the results of the particular substantive test being undertaken.

One final consideration for an internal audit situation is the
accuracy of the budgeted figures, as mentioned above, if these
are to be used. It is possible that a budgeted population figure
may turn out to be seriously inaccurate, and the auditor will
find the sample chosen too large or too small in the formula for
sample size used above. This formula can of course be
rearranged.

sample size = pop. × rel. fac. / precision
    precision = pop × rel. fac. / sample size
              = pop × rel. fac. / (pop / sampling interval)
              = rel. fac. × sampling interval

This is a useful relationship to remember when evaluating results,
but it is the sampling interval that is useful at the moment.

So, although the final sample size may not be known at the
start, the sampling interval can be calculated. For planning purposes this will indicate the frequency of testing throughout the
year, or for any other period of system operation, and is usually
just as convenient.

From the last relationship above,

Sampling interval = precision (UEL, MTEL) / reliability factor

In this case

£500 000 / 1.39 = every £359 712nd

This is after choosing a random start or other random selection
method already described.

If the population did in fact turn out to equal the last population figure used above, then every £359 712nd interval would

still give the same sample size, (£20 080 000 / £359 712 = 55.8, say, 56).

Conclusion

Monetary unit sampling is far superior to most other approaches for monetary conclusions required in most audit testing situations. Although it offers a very powerful audit tool, its use must be carefully planned. Key items should be extracted as far as possible, and the internal auditor in particular may benefit from consulting management about the sampling parameters to be used.

Because MUS tends to be used in substantive testing, it is sometimes seen as an expensive technique, though in practice this would be just as problematical if a non-statistical approach were used and the sample were large enough to be representative of the population.

MUS tends to be efficient only when relatively few errors are anticipated, and so it is best used on large populations that the auditor feels are likely to be reasonably accurate, but where he needs to form a measurable conclusion about this. MUS also tends to be less efficient for spotting underpayments, for example, income not collected. Of course, this last problem is true of testing generally, and quite often auditors would use analytical review techniques, or take separate measures to ensure that the population is complete, or test a related population that is known to be complete, rather than expect to spot missing amounts when the main risk is that the population tested will exclude income not recorded. Underpayments can of course come to light when one is testing, even if the main risk is of overpayments, and as we shall see in the next chapter it is best to evaluate over- and underpayments separately.

Although no hard and fast rules can be given, the following expenditure balances/systems are examples which are potentially suitable for MUS:

- Payrolls.
- Creditors/purchasing.

- Fees.
- Regular contract revenue expenses.
- Stocks and stores.
- Travel and subsistence payments.
- Claims (insurance or benefits).
- Grants.
- Capital works payments.
- Loan repayments.
- Investments.

In general, the judgment needed in internal audits using MUS are likely to result in a wider variation in parameters, particularly precision (that is, materiality) than similar situations for an external audit.

7 Monetary unit sampling – taking account of errors

One of the main practical problems of leaving MUS at the point reached in the previous chapter is that any error will mean the parameters chosen have not held. In theory, this is no worse a situation than for the compliance testing discussed in Chapter 5. One could reassess the parameters (recalculate the risk/confidence for the planned materiality or calculate a revised materiality for initial parameters), or undertake a larger sample allowing for 1, 2, 3 errors, and so on.

In practice, however, the costs of more sampling and the embarrassment(?) of agreeing new parameters, that is, the inconvenience in general of finding unexpected substantive test errors in a 'tightly' planned situation, may well lead auditors to consider building in a 'safety margin' at the planning stage, even though this may result in a slightly larger sample.

Two options

This situation is perhaps best seen as presenting two options.

1   The first option considers whether the level of materiality

chosen is likely to be breached if the other parameters of risk/confidence are retained.

2   The second option considers what new level of risk/confidence can be associated with the errors discovered for the planned level of materiality.

(From *Statistics for Audit*, CIPFA, 1995 p. 47)

It is usually more convenient to accept a slightly larger sample size at the start than to face negotiations over previously agreed parameters, extra work, or the prospect of appearing to 'fix new parameters to fit the results'. In internal audits, or large scale external audits, it can be particularly embarrassing and inefficient to have to go back on parameters agreed after lengthy discussion with senior client managers over the acceptable sample size, risk, precision and time to be spent on the audit, and to suggest that they either accept new parameters, or reject the population. (Even when they have been warned that this may be necessary, many auditees express considerable scepticism.)

Thus we have assumed that the more strict Option 1 above will be followed, but allowing for a safety margin as shown below.

(Some auditors may wish to pursue Option 2, particularly in an external audit situation where client managers have not been involved in discussions of testing parameters, and the auditor will merely give a brief audit opinion in generalized, non-specific terms. For Option 2 readers are referred to the coverage in the above-mentioned CIPFA publication and perhaps to seek further expert statistical advice.)

The safety margin and precision gap widening

The 'safety margin' is most easily seen as taking a precision level slightly more demanding (that is, lower) than the level of materiality or maximum tolerable error level which you are really prepared to accept.

Figure 7.1 shows bars representing the monetary value of the chosen materiality or MTEL. One can add or deduct amounts from this limit, or simply use the full amount as the denominator in the sample size formula, p. 54. Certainly, auditors can at least plan for a level of anticipated error (AE) in the population, based on past experience. A level of basic precision (BP), that in addition to any AE still falls short of the materiality, will be planned for.

In reality, if more than anticipated errors are found, the level of planned precision used in the formula will need to be expanded, that is, increased to make a less precise statement. This is referred to as precision gap widening (PGW), the formula for which is given below in Figure 7.1.

Following the results of the audit any PGW (which decreases the precision) will move the projected upper error level UEL

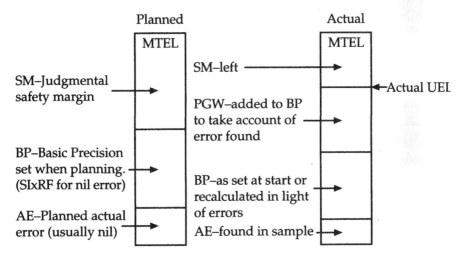

NB: Not to scale.
PGW is measured as the difference between the reliability factors (RF) at a given confidence level, less one, for each increasing error, i.e.

$$PGW = (b - a) - 1 \text{ where:}$$
$$a = RF \text{ for } x \text{ error, e.g. nil error}$$
$$b = RF \text{ for } x + 1 \text{ error, e.g. 1st error found}$$

For example, at 95% confidence level, for nil anticipated error, the first error found/ranked in the sample would require a PGW factor of
$(4.75 - 3.00) - 1 = 0.75$.

Figure 7.1   Precision gap widening

closer to the materiality. In a well-planned audit, however, the eventual projected UEL should remain below materiality or MTEL, so enabling the auditor to conclude that the chosen parameters have held. In fact, the auditor could conclude that the actual UEL projected was the extrapolated error in the population at the chosen confidence and risk. However, if errors are so much more than expected that the PGW brings the UEL beyond the MTEL, the managers should be warned that the auditors consider the risk of a material error to be unacceptable, or that the system output is likely to be unreliable to a significant degree, possibly quoting the parameters and MTEL used for testing.

The mechanics of extrapolation

Some people find this a rather tedious topic, and it is only fair to concede that current, widely-available (and relatively inexpensive) audit software not only calculates the sample size and other planning options and prints out the sample from downloaded data, but also provides instant evaluations and extrapolation of errors to the population. Even so, we feel that it is worth understanding how this can actually be done as part of the wider background knowledge often expected of auditors, particularly from interested clients. The credibility of auditors is often put under more strain than other professions by stock answers along the lines of 'it's a mystery to me, it all goes on inside the machine'.

More than one possible series of steps can be used, as was apparent in our earlier discussions (Chapter 4 and the start of this chapter). Different approaches have been outlined by various experts, but the approach described below takes account of existing guidance published by the UK accountancy bodies without following it in any slavish fashion, for example, in respect of Option 2.

Three main stages of MUS extrapolation
Basically there are three main stages involved in Option 1, page 67:

1 Estimating the most likely error (MLE).
2 Adjusting the basic precision by an amount of PGW.
3 Comparing the MLE plus the final precision level (the final UEL) to the chosen materiality or MTEL.

It is worth noting at this juncture that, if Option 2 (p. 68) had been followed, we might well have had to choose new parameters of confidence and risk about the likelihood of a material error level existing in the population.

Some auditors are tempted simply to compare the MLE to the MTEL, ignoring precision. This is not advisable, because of the incomplete nature of the statistical conclusion (see pages 31–2) and the fact that it would leave the auditor open to the accusation that senior client managers had been misled with a less than complete report. Saying, for example, that you are 95 per cent confident that the most likely error is £x and this is less than MTEL, without saying that it might be much more than £x (by the upper precision level), or that there is a high risk of it being more than £x, is hardly likely to place you in a credible position if unacceptable errors subsequently come to light!

Figure 7.2(a) below presents a suggested work sheet for extrapolation, to which you may refer as we go through the steps in more detail.

Before starting, it is usually helpful to have separate sheets available for over- and understatement errors, because these should be evaluated separately for Option 1.

1 Start by calculating the 'tainting' proportion of each error – error/book value – (columns A to D of the work sheet) to taint the proportion of the book value of the sample in error. (*N.B.* Tainting should always be less than 1 for this approach.)
2 To be prudent and to maximize the estimated error as we go along, these taintings should be ranked in descending order highest value first (column E). These tainted amounts are then multiplied by the sampling interval (column F) to find the projected error (column G). The total of this column (subject to any adjustments from column L, see step 5) is the most likely error (MLE), the first of the three main stages mentioned above.

OVER/UNDERSTATEMENTS* COMBINED EVALUATION SHEET

Error No.	A Recorded Value £	B Audited Value £	C Over/Under-statement Errors (A − B)	D Tainting % (C/A)	E Ranking (Highest First)	F Sampling Interval	G Projectal Error £ (D × F)

NOTES: *   Delete as appropriate and use separate sheets for over- and understatements.

       **   This column can be ignored if nil errors were anticipated and the book value of population was accurately known at the planning stage.

               Column 1 can then be taken simply as a basic precision chosen.

               (If the final UEL is just over materiality check that the value of column I would not have been reduced by using columns H × F where column F was calculated without rounding up.)

       ***   This can be calculated using the formula. PGW Factor = (reliability factor for current error − reliability factor for previous at nil errors) − 1.

Figure 7.2(a)   MUS Evaluation Sheet

H** Reliability Factor for Nil Errors	I Basic Precision £ (F × H)	J*** PGW Factor (from tables)	K PGW £ (D × F × J)	L 'Key' Item Errors £	M Most Likely Error (MLE) £ (G + L)	N Upper Error Limit (UEL) £ (I + K + M)	Comments

N.B. When drafting a final conclusion the auditor must remember to:-

i) Add or deduct the net value of the errors discovered (C + L) from the value of the final population.

ii) Deduct overstatement errors from the value of the UEL for overstatement and understatement errors from the UEL for understatements (columns C and N).

iii) Include in the wording of the conclusion the net MLE (M) as the point estimate, the chosen confidence level and the UELs (N) as the range of precision.

3   So far we have arrived at a point estimate; now we need the precision (see p. 31 if you are unsure about this concept). We include the 'basic precision' (chosen at the start of the audit, assuming nil errors and fitted into the formula on p. 54 to calculate sample size, that is, population × reliability factor/precision). This precision can be included directly in most cases (into column I). If the population was not known at the start or has been significantly adjusted, then the basic precision can be calculated using the relationship set out on p. 63, that is, reliability factor × sampling interval (columns H × F). Note that roundings used in the calculation of sample size and sampling interval, plus the fact that the reliability factors are themselves rounded figures, can give slight variations in basic precision, but these are rarely sufficient to influence the final conclusion.

4   To the basic precision needs to be added the precision gap widening (PGW) as explained on p. 68, to allow for the expansion of precision caused by the finding of more than expected error. Although tables of factors used for PGW are available, the formula given below and on the work sheet is not usually inconvenient to use for a small number of errors.

PGW factor = (RF for current error − RF for previous error) − 1

The PGW factor (inserted into column J) is multiplied against the tainting and the sampling interval to give the total PGW (column K). This completes the second of the three main stages on p. 70.

5   We are now ready to form our conclusion but, before we do so, we must take into account 'key' items – those, if any, taken out before sampling and tested 100 per cent (explained on p. 56). If any errors are found, these can be added directly to our point estimate (columns L & M).

6   Finally, we are in a position to add up the component results of our extrapolation – that is, MLE, Precision and PGW – to form our projected UEL (column N). This we hope will be less than our materiality or MTEL, and some of

the safety margin introduced during audit planning will remain. If not, we and our audited client managers have every reason to be concerned. Even at this late stage auditors may feel they can use professional judgments about how far over the MTEL the UEL lies and what the final risk implications are, although in this book we would advise extreme caution before overriding initial parameters chosen and agreed with senior client managers.

Let's look at a case study illustrating these stages.

Case study 5: MUS with overpayment error

As we pointed out earlier, MUS is generally more suited to testing for over- rather than underpayment or where the main risk is of overpayment. (Though underpayment can be accommodated, as outlined in Case Study 7, p. 82.)

A payroll audit is under way on an annual weekly payroll output of £21 985 990. Most weekly staff work in unsocial conditions and earn around £450 per week. The maximum tolerable error level, agreed following a report to the audit committee, is set in relation to the organization's total budget and accounts at £1 100 000. The auditor wants to be 95 per cent confident that this level is not breached on this audit and, following regular compliance testing plus previous years' substantive testing, feels justified in allowing for nil errors from the sample. For testing purposes precision is set at £1 000 000, leaving a safety margin of £100 000.

The sample size is 65.96 say, 66 (£21 985 990 × 3 / £1 000 000)

Note: if no safety margin had been introduced, the sample size would have been 60 (£21 985 990 × 3 / £1 100 000).

Sampling interval is £333 121 06 (£21 985 990 / 66) (say £333 121).

The audit proceeds as usual with detailed substantive testing of the accuracy, validity and completeness of payroll payments, and everything goes as planned until one payment of £464.20 is found to be £11.20 over, due to simple miscasting.

Consider the implications of this error for the MTEL chosen (see Figure 7.2(b)).

Suggestions

The extrapolated UEL in the population is far below the MTEL, so at this point the auditor is not very concerned about the error. If no more errors are discovered (as is likely considering none were expected), then for the small cost of testing six more items than would have been so (66–60, see above) the safety margin has held. This has saved the auditor the hassle and cost of re-evaluating parameters, particularly risk and MTEL, that have already been agreed as acceptable, and, even worse, of resampling.

Note that, had the basic precision needed to be calculated using column H, the rounding up to 66 in the calculation of sample size would have to be ignored to arrive at the sampling interval, leading to a precision of £1 000 000. (£21 985 990 / 65.95797 = £333 333.33, not £333 121).

But what if the population was worse than expected? In particular, what if it contained some larger errors? We shall look at this situation in the next case study.

Case study 6: MUS overpayments extrapolated beyond MTEL

Consider the implications if, in the previous case, a second overpayment of £126.00 on a relatively large payment of £526 was discovered (see Figure 7.2(c)).

Suggestions

In this case note that the ranking of the tainting percentages is now changed, and this affects the PGW formerly calculated for the previous error.

It is not so much the size of the error that is important as its tainting, particularly when many similarly-sized transactions are being audited. If the taintings are all small, then perhaps several errors can be tolerated where no single one may be enough to cause concern.

The auditor notes that the UEL now exceeds the MTEL and by the fairly large margin of £52 303! It is difficult to form anything other than a negative conclusion, however it is phrased. Certainly the auditor cannot be 95 per cent confident that a material error is absent on the payroll.

In practice, the findings from other audit work both on this system and balance and on other areas within the organization may have a bearing. For example, the following are likely to be considered in a situation such as this where the MTEL has been breached.

Given the expectation of no errors being discovered, the presence of two in only a relatively small sample may well cause concern over the initial confidence with which the system was viewed. Were the compliance tests adequate, for example?

This provides an illustration of the 'needle in a haystack' situation where a worrying and relatively large error was found from 'favouring' the largish value transactions. If transactions on a conventional non-monetary basis had all had an equal chance of selection, the chances of the second error being hit would have been reduced.

Irrespective of the sampling technique, the auditor will, naturally, consider the causes of the errors: are they simply a coincidence of unavoidable human error or is some fundamental flaw at work in the system? New procedures, perhaps, or a cutback in supervision, or poor training, or the recruitment of a particular person lacking in competence, and so on?

Whatever is finally concluded, it is clear at this point that further testing will be required. Should this be done by the client or by audit staff?

MUS is relatively intolerant of errors and a prudent approach has been followed, so it is not surprising that the second error breaches MTEL. In fact, if it had been discovered first, the same conclusions would have been reached after one error, although, if a second or even third error had been of a small tainting like

OVER/UNDERSTATEMENTS* COMBINED EVALUATION SHEET

Error No.	A Recorded Value £	B Audited Value £	C Over/Under-statement Errors (A − B)	D Tainting % (C/A)	E Ranking (Highest First)	F Sampling Interval	G Projectal Error £ (D × F)
1	464.20	453.00	11.20	$\dfrac{11.20}{464.20}$ = 2.4%	1st	333,121	333,121 × 0.024 = 7,994.90

NOTES: *   Delete as appropriate and use separate sheets for over- and understatements.

       **   This column can be ignored if nil errors were anticipated and the book value of population was accurately known at the planning stage.
Column 1 can then be taken simply as basic precision chosen.
(If the final UEL is just over materiality check that the value of column I would not have been reduced by using columns H × F where column F was calculated without rounding up.)

      ***   This can be calculated using the formula. PGW Factor = (reliability factor for current error − reliability factor for previous at nil errors) − 1 = (4.75 − 3.0) − 1 = 0.75. (for 1st error)

Figure 7.2(b)   MUS Evaluation Sheet

H** Reliability Factor for Nil Errors	I Basic Precision £ (F × H)	J*** PGW Factor (from tables)	K PGW £ (D × F × J)	L 'Key' Item Errors £	M Most Likely Error (MLE) £ (G + L)	N Upper Error Limit (UEL) £ (I + K + M)	Comments
–	1,000,000	0.75	0.024 × 333,121 × 0.75 = 5,996.18	NIL	7,994.90	1,000,000 5,996 7,995 1,013,991	UEL is less than MTEL

N.B. When drafting a final conclusion the auditor must remember to:-
i) Add or deduct the net value of the errors discovered (C + L) from the value of the final population.
ii) Deduct overstatement errors from the value of the UEL for overstatement and understatement errors from the UEL for understatements (columns C and N).
iii) Include in the wording of the conclusion the net MLE (M) as the point estimate, the chosen confidence level and the UELs (N) as the range of precision.

OVER/UNDERSTATEMENTS* COMBINED EVALUATION SHEET

Error No.	A Recorded Value £	B Audited Value £	C Over/Under-statement Errors (A − B)	D Tainting % (C/A)	E Ranking (Highest First)	F Sampling Interval	G Projectal Error £ (D × F)
1.	464.20	453.00	11.20	2.4%	2nd	333,121	7,995
2.	526.00	400.00	126.00	24%	1st	333,121	79,949

NOTES: *   Delete as appropriate and use separate sheets for over- and understatements.

       **   This column can be ignored if nil errors were anticipated and the book value of population was accurately known at the planning stage.

            Column 1 can then be taken simply as basic precision chosen.

            (If the final UEL is just over materiality check that the value of column I would not have been reduced by using columns H × F where column F was calculated without rounding up.)

       ***   This can be calculated using the formula. PGW Factor = (reliability factor for current error − reliability factor for previous at nil errors) − 1 = (4.75 − 3.0) − 1 = 0.75. (for 1st error)

Figure 7.2(c)   MUS Evaluation Sheet

H** Reliability Factor for Nil Errors	I Basic Precision £ (F × H)	J*** PGW Factor (from tables)	K PGW £ (D × F × J)	L 'Key' Item Errors ·£	M Most Likely Error (MLE) £ (G + L)	N Upper Error Limit (UEL) £ (I + K + M)	Comments
—	1,000,000	0.55	4,397 [0.024 × 333,121 × 0.55]	NIL	7,995	1,000,000 64,359 87,944	
—	1,000,000	0.75	59,962 [0.24 × 333,121 × 0.75]		79,949		
			64,359	NIL	87,944	1,152,303	UEL more than MTEL

N.B. When drafting a final conclusion the auditor must remember to:-

i) Add or deduct the net value of the errors discovered (C + L) from the value of the final population.

ii) Deduct overstatement errors from the value of the UEL for overstatement and understatement errors from the UEL for understatements (columns C and N).

iii) Include in the wording of the conclusion the net MLE (M) as the point estimate, the chosen confidence level and the UELs (N) as the range of precision.

the first, the UEL might still have remained below MTEL and this is, perhaps, the more usual situation. In practice, experienced auditors (despite increasing the sample size by introducing a safety margin) may form a more accurate initial impression of the soundness of the system than the one illustrated by this case.

Case study 7: MUS with over- and underpayment error

We have already stressed the disadvantages of using MUS to detect underpayments; nevertheless, underpayments can occur on balances and systems being tested mainly for risk of overpayments. Payroll is a typical example: quite often the payees will not spot small underpayments and unlike in the case of, say, creditors, there is less of an inbuilt tendency for these errors to be corrected shortly after payment has taken place.

Continuing to use the parameters set out in Case Study 5, assume the first error discovered in this case study was followed by an underpayment of £9 on a payment of £411 (but not the second overpayment considered in the last case study).

For the sake of illustration also assume that key items had already been extracted from the payroll before arriving at the total of £21 985 990 (it is not necessary to know their value for our purposes of extrapolation, just that they were tested 100 per cent). Errors in these items amounting to £300 overpayment were found.

Consider the extrapolation of errors to the population (see Figure 7.2(d)).

Suggestions
The first consideration is a matter of principle: when, if at all, should we net off the over- and underpayments?

Should we use two separate extrapolations and go on to report two separate conclusions? Some auditors prefer to do this, because the chances of finding understatements are inherently lower than overstatements and the implications may be viewed differently.

Should we net off the over- and understatements to find the net MLE? This often seems a sound option, but what about the precision limits? It does not follow that these should be netted off, as it is logical to talk separately about an UEL for 'unders' and an UEL for 'overs'.

We shall set out the conclusion so that you can choose between these two suggestions to suit your own audit situations.

Clearly, without the large error and tainting of the previous case study the UELs cannot threaten the MTEL. It has been assumed that the auditor is more interested in overpayments of payroll, although some organizations would find any accusation of underpaying staff just as embarrassing, even though underpayments are unlikely to be widespread.

In this case it may be more helpful to restate the findings from column N as:

- To nearest £1.
- Net MLE £966 (£300 + 7 995 − 7 329).
- UEL of overpayments £1 014 291 (BP + PGW + MLE for overs).
- UEL of underpayments £1 012 825 (BP + PGW + MLE for unders).

Conclusion

Substantive testing is expensive and, although MUS optimizes the sample size to fit the professional judgments about acceptable parameters right at the start of the audit, the possibility of a minor error or two leading you to retest or reassess the chosen parameters makes it worth introducing a safety margin.

The temptation to revise the MTEL, acceptable risk, or other parameters, particularly if these have been agreed at a senior level at the start of the audit, should be avoided as far as

OVER/UNDERSTATEMENTS* COMBINED EVALUATION SHEET

Error No.	A Recorded Value £	B Audited Value £	C Over/Under-statement Errors (A − B)	D Tainting % (C/A)	E Ranking (Highest First)	F Sampling Interval	G Projectal Error £ (D × F)
OVERS	464.20	453.00	11.20	2.4%	1st	333,121	7,995
UNDERS	411.00	420.00	9.00	2.2%	1st	333,121	7,329

NOTES: * Delete as appropriate and use separate sheets for over- and understatements.
– for the sake of illustration and comparison one sheet is used for both in this example.
** This column can be ignored if nil errors were anticipated and the book value of population was accurately known at the planning stage.
Column 1 can then be taken simply as basic precision chosen.
(If the final UEL is just over materiality check that the value of column I would not have been reduced by using columns H × F where column F was calculated without rounding up.)
*** This can be calculated using the formula. PGW Factor = (reliability factor for current error − reliability factor for previous at nil errors) − 1.

Figure 7.2(d)   MUS Evaluation Sheet

H** Reliability Factor for Nil Errors	I Basic Precision £ (F × H)	J*** PGW Factor (from tables)	K PGW £ (D × F × J)	L 'Key' Item Errors £	M Most Likely Error (MLE) £ (G + L)	N Upper Error Limit (UEL) £ (I + K + M)	Comments
	1,000,000	0.75	5,996	300	8,295	1,000,000 5,996 8,295	OVER UEL = 1,014,291 ie less than MTEL for OVERS
	1,000,000	0.75	5,496 [0.022 × 333,121 × 0.75]	NIL	7329 966 NET	1,000,000 5,496 7,329	UNDER UEL = 1,012,825 ie less than MTEL for UNDERS

N.B. When drafting a final conclusion the auditor must remember to:-
i)   Add or deduct the net value of the errors discovered (C + L) from the value of the final population.
ii)   Deduct overstatement errors from the value of the UEL for overstatement and understatement errors from the UEL for understatements (columns C and N).
iii) Include in the wording of the conclusion the net MLE (M) as the point estimate, the chosen confidence level and the UELs (N) as the range of precision.

possible, unless there has been a genuine change in the factors that first led you to judge the acceptability of such parameters.

In general, any serious risk of underpayment remaining undetected should lead to separate audit evidence to back up any sampling rather than relying on MUS. Certainly, for income the auditor will need evidence of completeness of system output from other sources such as analytical review, compliance testing of sales, income recording and collection systems, observation, and so on.

Nevertheless, the use of MUS offers a much improved and more justifiable method than haphazard, basic attribute sampling, or selective judgmental approaches. For many service-based organizations with high staff costs, massive paper-processing systems such as claims payments, or public services that basically spend money allocated from taxation, MUS offers an exceptionally powerful audit tool.

8 Risk models and the reduction of sample sizes

We have already discussed how sample sizes may be reduced by taking an organization-wide view of materiality (see the discussions in Case Study 4). Taking full account of risk analysis can also reduce sample sizes as well as being an essential component of audit planning and management. It is important to stress that this is not a text about risk management or risk analysis. This chapter only takes account of the subject in sufficient detail to explain some of the practical uses for the audit sampling techniques discussed in earlier chapters.

It is important to remain aware of the caution raised earlier, p. 26, in effect, that an appearance of mathematical exactitude can lull the unwary into a false sense of security. This is often so with risk models. Although the laws of probability or other mathematical approaches may be implied in their construction and use, risk is essentially a rather subjective concept. Most of the percentage values or other values included in such models are based more on subjective judgment than on precise measurement. Nevertheless, risk models greatly encourage the consistent application of such judgments across the range of audits and facilitate the documentation of otherwise scantily explained or recorded allocation of risk.

We have been using the concept of risk simply as the converse of confidence. Assuming, however, that the auditor chooses to arrive at a judgment about risk and confidence levels, this can be taken as given for the purpose of audit sampling. In one sense this is a matter of practicality: the number of possible risk models, not to mention the range of professional judgments, in any one complex organization is simply vast and certainly beyond the scope of a short book such as this. But it is also worth pointing out ways that the use of risk models in general, and the approach promulgated by SAS 300 in particular, can help reduce sample size by facilitating some of the confidence and risk to be taken from sources of audit evidence, other than the results of one particular sample.

Taking continuous account, or at least regular appraisal, of all sources of evidence is after all no more than common sense and what happens on a judgmental basis, with or without any formal risk model. At various points in the case studies we have accepted that auditors will take account of the reliability of the system, particularly the results of compliance testing of internal control, when deciding the risk of error in the population and translating this into judgment about the level of substantive testing. If, say, we have already formed the opinion that a system is well designed, if we have the results of compliance testing indicating that the controls were soundly operated over the whole period being audited (population), we would normally be inclined to accept a smaller sample for relatively expensive substantive testing than if we had no evidence of control, or evidence of poor control.

We would in effect be accepting a lower confidence level and higher risk for substantive testing because some of our confidence comes from compliance testing and other audit sources. See also the discussion on pp. 51–3 regarding MUS and the role of substantive testing.

As auditors we might simply use our judgment in such matters, or we might use a more formal risk model, or both: as pointed out above there are many variations of these. The 'total audit risk' model, which we will consider a little later on in this chapter, is perhaps the most widely applicable at present, has a history of acceptance by many authorities and is broadly in line with SAS 300.

This model also has the distinct advantage of being relatively straightforward in concept (no long algebraic-style formulas full of different weightings so popular in the past) and it uses categories consistent with the broad stages of a typical systems-based audit. As we shall see, the use of the model is particularly convenient for subdividing the reliability factor among the different sources of audit evidence. It is the division of the reliability factor between sources of evidence (that is, of audit assurance) that enables the sample sizes to be reduced by, in turn, reducing the numerator in the formula used in previous chapters (sample size = population × reliability factor / precision).

But, before we look at the total audit risk model in detail, it may help to analyse exactly what we mean by 'risk' and even what is meant by the well-entrenched term 'internal control'.

Risk of what?

Auditors sometimes treat the identification of risk as an end in itself or, even worse, they may unquestioningly take on board established practices, notably published lists of risks and internal controls.

Perhaps we see past best practice simply as something to follow or copy rather than as advice. Unfortunately, risk is not this simple. In terms of auditing and managing an organization a risk exists insofar as it can affect your objectives. Any potential threat to objectives including meeting regulatory requirements is a risk. But both the business objectives and quite often the regulatory ones are in a nearly constant state of flux at different levels throughout the organization. Auditors who rely on established lists and published best practice in identifying the current risks to an organization are skating on very thin ice. When identifying risk, we must constantly refer back to the business objectives and ask ourselves what threatens or could threaten these.

Controls are seen in terms of their ability to guard against risk, though the same bad habits of slavishly following past practice can apply to internal control. The main financial systems tend to have a lot of accounting procedures and administrative arrangements in common and so, traditionally, internal control is seen merely in terms of standard arrangements that vary little from one organization to another (bank reconciliation, payment authorization, separations of duties, and so on). Often standard control listings, including standard objectives and audit tests, are available, even to fairly junior auditors. At best this situation ensures that minimum 'typical' risks are guarded against. At worst, it can induce complacency, a by-the-book-attitude, which is most unlikely to guard against the latest business risk.

A simple triangular relationship

The relationship below (Figure 8.1) is well worth considering at the start of each audit and certainly when analysing risk. In even the most conventional of financial systems within the most stable of business environments, changes in markets, financial instruments, policy, and so on, can have an unpredictable effect upon the working arrangements needed to guard against risk. In more fluid situations and non-financial systems this is even more the case.

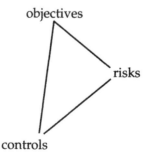

Figure 8.1   Objectives, risks and controls

It might be argued that a more linear relationship with objectives at the top, followed by risks, followed by controls, is more appropriate, without a direct link between controls and objectives. However, as the 'COSO' report (see Appendix 6) puts it:

Establishment of objectives is a precondition to internal control . . .

This relationship recognizes that internal control is often viewed directly as any arrangement or procedure that ensures that an objective will be met, or without which it may be threatened. Clearly this implies a degree of risk analysis, but it is often more helpful to consider the three elements together, as all being interrelated, rather than as a dependent linear progression. Few people can spot all the risks without also considering controls, or controls without considering risks, or either without considering objectives, and it can be rather inefficient to work out the risks, find a control that does not appear to guard against the risks you have listed, only then to realize (assuming it relates to an objective) that this means you have missed one of the risks.

Despite the benefits of the simple relationship in Figure 8.1, all too often one comes across managers and auditors considering each of the three elements above in isolation. Sometimes senior managers set objectives, call in consultants to analyse the risk, and leave the identification of internal control to the auditor – without any formal arrangement to compare the different results!

Using 'nightmare' scenarios to identify key risks

Surprisingly, perhaps one of the most difficult aspects of risk analysis is gaining consensus about the objectives. Large organizations with different levels of management and different units within the same body, not always pursuing harmonious objectives, can present the auditor with unsynchronized, even conflicting, objectives at any one time. Worse, management responsible for a particular system may have no clear understanding of its objectives, and may not even have thought of the particular duties about which the auditor is concerned as a 'system' at all, merely as an (unrelated) selection of their wider span of duties and responsibilities. Take, for example, a stores manager, whose daily objectives include: the physical security of the building; ensuring customers are served without delay; ensuring stock lines do not run out or below preset reorder levels; maintaining the correct temperatures, humidities, and so on. How will this manager view the auditor's perception of a stock-management system's objectives as ensuring the accuracy of the stores records compared to stock held? This will at best be one among many of the manager's objectives, and he may view his operations in terms of the above objectives, among which the promptness and accuracy of keying in records, while not being totally unimportant, may rank a good deal lower than not spoiling particular lines. Clearly, a good system will cover more than one objective, but the priority implied by an auditor's judgment of system objectives may not immediately be understood and agreed by the manager.

How is the auditor to begin meaningful discussion of objectives and risks relating to the system under audit, without imposing 'audit' views, which often miss some key concern because of the auditor's own inexperience or experience of 'other people's' systems?

Often the best starting-point is to ask key control issues, or 'nightmare scenarios' which are designed to elucidate:

1   whether the manager agrees about the seriousness of what the auditor considers to be a 'nightmare' – in which case the objectives and risks start to become clearer;
2   what procedures or arrangements actually prevent such a nightmare – that is, what the key controls are in the system.

Such nightmare scenarios are sometimes called 'key control questions' by auditors who tend to limit their initial system evaluation to identifying the essential minimum of risks and related controls. Key control questions are best put bluntly and simply. A definite 'yes' or 'no', followed by no more than a short explanation, is the desired response. Often it is easier to put the questions so that a 'no' is expected. The following sets out a typical example relating to a system that is likely to be familiar to most auditors – purchasing.

Typical key control questions – purchasing system
Can any unnecessary purchases be made?
No, only budget holders are allowed to initiate purchases. Each budget holder signs a purchase request confirming the goods are required for a specified need. Amounts over £xxx are countersigned by Head of Department.

Can any unauthorized purchases be made?
No, the central Purchasing Officer checks each request to confirm it has been signed by a budget holder and he/she then signs the form filling in the official order number and details at the bottom. All purchases are then made by official order cross referenced to the purchase request. The order form states it is invalid unless signed and dated by the Purchasing Officer. The Purchasing Officer is not a budget holder.

Can incorrect purchase details remain uncorrected?
No, the Purchasing Officer sends a copy order back to the budget holder before it is posted out who signs it to confirm details are correct and the purchase still valid, before forwarding to accounts branch who will make payment. There is rarely any problem sorting out ordering discrepancies so long as payment has not been made.

This is the sort of information that enables the auditor to start documenting the system and identifying its key controls.

KCQs are usually few in number for any one system, few systems have more than one or two main purposes and five or six are unusually complex. They work best when worded to concentrate the recipient's mind on the most obvious and serious purposes of the system.

The total audit risk model

Once the auditor has identified the risks, the more difficult task of analysis begins. How significant are the risks? At this point the auditor and the manager may diverge, at least partly. Most managers are primarily concerned with the potential impacts and consequences of the risk – what will it mean for their workload, their department, organization, future, and so on? A qualitative prioritization is usually sufficient to meet such concerns and, following on from this, responsible managers will try to ensure that an adequate set of internal controls is in place to minimize such risks.

Auditors will certainly need to take account of the foregoing, essentially management, analysis and this can usually be achieved at a strategic level by prioritizing assignments in harmony with managerial risk priorities. But most audit (and some management) risk analysis goes beyond this stage to arrive at a conclusion on the risk of the impact occurring. In financial systems this is in effect the risk of:

- an error (monetary or control deviation) occurring, that is, 'inherent risk' (IR);
- an error occurring and not being corrected by controls at some stage in the system, that is, the 'control risk' (CR);
- an error occurring, not being corrected by controls and not being detected by the audit testing, that is, 'detection risk' (DR).

In fact these three very broad categories may be subdivided to isolate, say, the control environment from the quality of designed control, or to split testing between the particular tests being planned and other audit tests, and so on. But for the sake of reasonable simplicity we will limit our consideration to the three broad categories just outlined.

SAS 300 uses and builds upon this approach and categorizes the total risk of the audit, or the audit risk (AR) as the product of the three (or however many you use) categories:

$$AR = IR \times CR \times DR$$

Conceptually, this model is rather like a series of filters: all transactions are filtered through the initial checking and processing system, but a small percentage of items might be erroneous; some of these are filtered out by the controls; some are not, but of these some may be detected by testing. Like filters, additional layers of financial and quality management control can be present in different organizations, though we will keep to three basic levels in our model.

From an audit viewpoint the IR and CR can largely be taken as given. They will be indicated by such evidence as the initial system evaluation and the results of compliance testing. It is, however, only fair to point out that many of the 'local' or specific risk models that use long formulas, including factors such as transaction value, results of previous audits, experience of client staff, and so on, may be of help in forming an opinion on the IR and possibly even the CR. But as these cannot usually be altered in the short term, the auditor's attention will tend to focus upon the DR. The DR will depend very much on the level of testing, the resources the audited client is prepared to pay for, staff skills and factors that are the responsibility of the auditor and critical to his planning:

$$DR = AR \, / \, IR \times CR$$

Among the advantages of this model are the following:

1   Its congruence with the laws of probability and, thus, with the use of statistical sampling. In percentage or other measurable terms the AR represents the total risk the auditor judges is acceptable, 10 per cent, 0.1, and so on, and by definition the product of the other risk categories will come to the AR.
2   It can easily be divided into stages of audit evidence-gathering, the main stages that auditors tend to use when assessing the risk and confidence from different sources of audit evidence.
3   Following on from 1 and 2, the risk categories provide convenient divisions for confidence when assessing the level of testing required.

4   In practice, it is usually convenient to divide the reliability factor, which is the means of taking confidence/risk into account in our formula for sample size, between the categories on a pro rata basis. The methods of allocation will depend on judgment rather than statistical theory, but it is vital to use a consistent approach throughout. This can then provide a systematic and consistent approach to reducing the reliability factor, hence the sample size, using a widely-applicable risk model, as suggested in this chapter.

5   The auditor is not expected specifically to use quantitative methods to estimate the magnitude of risk in each category. From the standpoint of using the model it does not matter whether an inherent risk of, say, 90 per cent arises from a complex formula developed in-house by the auditors or from the experience and judgment of a particular auditor.

It may be helpful to look at some case studies at this juncture. Case Study 8 considers the use of the total audit risk model simply to illustrate how it might apply to audit management in general. Case Study 9 involves the use of the model in an audit-sampling context.

Case study 8: too much work!

This case is for illustration of the model rather than detailed consideration of any sampling implications or suggestions. Therefore, its content and format follow a more narrative style than the other case studies. Readers who are reasonably familiar with this approach to risk models may wish to proceed to the next case study.

Bill is Head of Internal Audit at a large corporation. He is considering whether or not his staff are performing too much or too little testing in various regular audit assignments, some of which are becoming increasingly costly.

Immediately before him is the senior auditor's summary of work and evaluation of past results relating to the monthly salary payroll system. The inherent risk is considered low for this system because all payments are by automatic bank transfer (BACS) and for relatively small amounts; the system is run by experienced staff, well-supervised and total payroll costs for this company are a relatively small proportion of operating cost.

The control risk is also thought to be low because the last six audits have concluded that internal controls are well-designed and soundly operated. Very few compliance testing errors have come to light.

Substantive testing is usually undertaken on a sample of ten payments each monthly run. This amounts to about 2 per cent of total payments by number, though less than $\frac{1}{2}$ per cent by value.

As a general rule Bill considers it prudent to aim for no more than 5 per cent risk that a material error could remain undetected on a year's transactions. In short, he likes to be very confident indeed that nothing unacceptable is likely on this main financial system and in *his* subjective judgment he aims for a 95 per cent confidence level, that is, an AR of 5 per cent.

First, Bill assumes there is a low risk of inherent error. Inherent risk is often put at 100 per cent because it is difficult to measure, especially for a new audit. In this case, however, payroll is small in relation to total costs and Bill judges that there is at most a 30 per cent inherent risk. He judges from the summary results prepared by his senior auditor that there is at most a 20 per cent risk of an error not being picked up by the internal controls. Given their current level of testing, he judges that there is a 50 per cent chance they will detect any material errors that do slip past the system. This is actually fairly good for audit testing, which often fails to pick up errors as a rule but, given that for an error to be material in this relatively small payroll it would have to be repeated on a wide scale or be something catastrophic such as the theft of an entire BACS transmission, Bill can afford to be fairly confident.

From the above we can see that Bill has kept his judgements on the prudent side, and yet he already has a lower level of DR than he strictly needs to give him the total AR he finds acceptable:

$$AR = 0.3 \times 0.2 \times 0.5 = 0.03 \text{ or } 3\% \text{ risk}$$

As a general rule Bill finds he can only afford to spend 1000 hours a year on substantive testing, unless special considerations come into play such as serious errors or fraud. Salaries are already taking up approximately 100 hours. If he reduced this to 50 hours, he would still be able to test about 1 per cent of the payroll volume and this he considers is more than sufficient and would he feels raise detection risk to, at most, 80 per cent.

In the model this would give:

$$AR = 0.3 \times 0.2 \times 0.8 = 0.048 \text{ or } 4.8\%$$

This is still below the 5 per cent AR level and, providing he has been cautious and erred on the prudent side in his judgements, should be acceptable.

If, for another system, say, creditors, Bill judged IR as 90 per cent, CR as 10 per cent, (a well-controlled system) and wanted to tolerate only a 5 per cent risk overall, what would an acceptable DR be for the particular test programme which he is about to ask his staff to carry out?

$$\begin{aligned} DR &= AR \, / \, IR.CR \\ &= 0.05 \, / \, 0.1 \times 0.9 \\ &= 55.6\% \end{aligned}$$

In effect Bill needs to ensure that his auditors undertake sufficient testing for him to be confident there would only be, say, a 55 per cent risk of not detecting an error or fraud of significance.

Case study 9: taking account of wider audit evidence

Henry, a senior internal auditor, is planning an audit of the claims-processing system and wishes to calculate a sample for substantive testing. He does not wish to take account of the materiality used for the organization as a whole, such as £2 000 000 used by the external auditors, as he intends reporting to the Director of Administration and senior line managers solely on their own responsibilities. A maximum tolerable error level has been agreed at £150 000 in relation to a year's claims of £15 000 000. It is usual in this organization for the internal auditor to adopt a 90 per cent confidence level and to leave a safety margin of 10 per cent of MTEL, so in this case reducing precision to £135 000 for testing purposes.

On the basis of past audit evidence, including recent compliance testing, Henry judges that no errors should be allowed for in substantive testing and will use a reliability factor of 2.31 for calculating sample size.

There is a definite risk of clerical error and he feels 100 per cent should be included in the inherent risk category. At first sight this may seem rather high, but he knows that a wide range of clerical errors is possible, and does not feel he can measure any reasonably accurate level of inherent risk so, to err on the side of caution, he assumes all transactions are a risk. Control risk he judges as 10 per cent – he has detailed reliable evidence that a sophisticated level of internal control is present in this system and very few deviations have been reported over the past few years.

Henry knows that his testing, on an MUS basis, will select the higher value items, though he has no sophisticated method of allocating risk to this. He assumes a 98 per cent DR as a general rule (98 per cent risk of not detecting an error) which he feels errs on the prudent side, as this takes no account of analytical review or other substantive tests. This gives an audit risk using the above model:

$$AR = IR \times CR \times DR$$

$$AR = 1.0 \times 0.1 \times 0.98 = 9.8\%$$

This is in fact slightly lower than the acceptable audit risk of 10 per cent, though one should continue to bear in mind that the model is not being used as a means of exact measurement. Its measurements are based entirely on professional judgments, the model itself merely providing a systematic approach to allocating risk.

If the AR had worked out higher than the acceptable 10 per cent level, additional audit work, internal control improvements, or improvement in the inherent design/management of the system, or a combination of these, would have been implied.

Consider:

1   The allocation of the reliability factor and sample size.
2   The effect of overpaying £230.00 in claim of £11 230.

Suggestions

On a simple pro rata basis 90 per cent of the reliability factor would be allocated to the internal control in the system and 10 per cent to the results of substantive testing. This would mean that a reliability factor of 2.31 would be split:

- 2.079 to internal control;
- 0.231 to substantive testing.

This would lead to a sample size for MUS testing of

$$\text{sample size} = (£15m \times 0.231) / £0.135m = 25.67 \text{ (i.e. 26)}$$

and

$$\text{sampling interval} = £15m / 26 = £576\ 923$$

In effect, Henry would be saying that he is prepared to accept 90 per cent of the 95 per cent confidence he is seeking for his audit conclusion to come from the level of internal control, and only 10 per cent of the 90 per cent from the results of substantive testing, and of course he is placing no reliance on the inherent nature of the system and its likelihood of error in the first place.

At this point it is likely that some people would question a simple pro rata basis, not because of any inconsistency in application of the model but simply because most auditors would be wary of placing too much reliance on indirect evidence such as compliance testing. Some auditors apply a policy of minimum assurance from direct evidence, say, 25 per cent. Thus, for a reliability factor of 2.31, whatever the theoretical assurance (confidence) that could be taken from other sources of evidence, a minimum reliability factor of 0.58 would be used. This would give a sample size of

$$\text{sample size} = 15 \times 0.58 / 0.135 = 64.44 \ (65)$$

$$\text{sampling interval} = \text{£15m} / 65 = \text{£230 769}$$

Given that a high degree of professional judgment is unavoidable, some would even question the need for a formal risk 'model' at all.

Perhaps a simple judgment on high-medium-low assurance could be translated into divisions of the total reliability factor that sum to 2.31, or 3.0 for 95 per cent confidence and nil error, or whatever factor is chosen? The risk in this approach is not that it is in any way invalid, but rather it may degenerate into a less consistent and less defensible position should one's professional judgment be questioned.

Other risk models, some more, others less, sophisticated than the one used in this case may well provide the best solution to your organization's audit needs. The critical point is not what is the best risk model, but that you should find a way of applying your judgments in a consistent and defensible manner, while at the same time using the optimal sample size implied from these judgments.

The effect of the overpayment is shown on the following work sheet, which is based on the first calculation of sample size and sampling interval above.

From this we can see that only a single error has taken Henry over the MTEL. The initial comments might be along the following lines.

Was the safety margin too narrow? Though a larger sample that a narrower margin would imply might have picked up more errors.

OVER/UNDERSTATEMENTS* COMBINED EVALUATION SHEET

Error No.	A Recorded Value £	B Audited Value £	C Over/Under-statement Errors (A − B)	D Tainting % (C/A)	E Ranking (Highest First)	F Sampling Interval	G Projectal Error £ (D × F)
1	11,230	11,000	230	2%	1st	576,923	11,538

NOTES: *   Delete as appropriate and use separate sheets for over- and understatements.
     ** This column can be ignored if nil errors were anticipated and the book value of population was accurately known at the planning stage.
Column 1 can then be taken simply as the basic precision chosen.
(If the final UEL is just over materiality check that the value of column I would not have been reduced by using columns H × F where column F was calculated without rounding up.)
    *** This can be calculated using the formula. PGW Factor = (reliability factor for current error − reliability factor for previous at nil errors) − 1.

Figure 8.2   Effect of overpayment

H** Reliability Factor for Nil Errors	I Basic Precision £ (F × H)	J*** PGW Factor (from tables)	K PGW £ (D × F × J)	L 'Key' Item Errors £	M Most Likely Error (MLE) £ (G + L)	N Upper Error Limit (UEL) £ (I + K + M)	Comments
—	135,000	0.75	8,653	NIL	11,538	135,000 8,653 11,538 15,5191	UEL is greater than MTEL

N.B. When drafting a final conclusion the auditor must remember to:-

i) Add or deduct the net value of the errors discovered (C + L) from the value of the final population.

ii) Deduct overstatement errors from the value of the UEL for overstatement and understatement errors from the UEL for understatements (columns C and N).

iii) Include in the wording of the conclusion the net MLE (M) as the point estimate, the chosen confidence level and the UELs (N) as the range of precision.

MUS is generally intolerant of errors and the smaller the sample size the less tolerant in general.

The tainting at 2 per cent is not all that small and the larger the tainting the more excessive the extrapolation.

In this particular case the UEL only exceeds the £150 000 by £5 191 or by 3.5 per cent and so one is bound to ask how strictly the senior managers actually view the MTEL: is it a fairly arbitrary figure, or was it 'fought over' before finally being agreed? The same questions would be asked in respect of risk and the allocation of the reliability factor. If these parameters are the very 'bottom line' that managers can accept, then this result is unacceptable and management checking or further audit is definitely required.

Overall, your attitude to planning and evaluating statistical sampling, particularly as the more complex techniques are used, depends on your organization's ethos, attitudes, conventions and view of what is best under changing circumstances. The sampling techniques provide an extremely powerful set of tools, but are absolutely no substitute for professional judgment.

Conclusion

However formal or informal our approach, we can not avoid forming professional judgments about risk, particularly at the strategic planning level and at the planning stage of each audit.

Perceptions of risk, and of controls, depend on objectives. In practice, the objectives of the organization from the corporate viewpoint change and they are not given equal importance throughout the organization between, say, different directors or business units. The nature of risk also varies, broadly speaking, between 'developmental' objectives such as those related to major expansion programmes, and 'maintenance' objectives such as many of the financial control objectives. The latter have traditionally dominated audit risk perceptions, but the former are becoming increasingly important to auditors particularly in respect of value-for-money audit and various management audits.

Formal risk models help ensure a consistent and defensible means of allocating audit resources, and the total audit risk model is one well-suited to transferring risk analysis results into simple arithmetical divisions of the reliability factor. Having said this, it is quite valid in principle to use less formalized professional judgment to allocate the risk/confidence into divisions of the reliability factor (as long as they sum to the total of the factor), provided you are consistent and objective in your judgments.

Reducing the reliability factor in this way merely takes account of assurance from different sources, which is also an unavoidable professional judgment. Internal auditors in particular may find this approach helpful when faced with client managers who, quite naturally, are more concerned about a relatively low MTEL in their systems than about the materiality level for the organization as a whole.

9 Other sampling approaches

In many respects this chapter is worth a book in its own right, but our aim is to provide a relatively short, practical text specifically for auditors, and a brief and selective overview will suffice.

Acceptance sampling

This is a particularly useful technique if auditors, at the strategic planning stage, or for whatever reason, are faced with a range of populations and wish to concentrate most of their efforts on systems with risk of unacceptable control deviation rates.

Usually a standard sample size is chosen simply in the light of time available, and the auditor rejects or accepts the sample depending on the UEL given by however many errors are found.

For example, it may be decided that the following range of results lead to the following actions.

A standard sample size of 50 control events (authorizations, separations, and so on) is chosen, and in the first sample

Table 9.1   Acceptance sampling

UEL	Action
5% or less	maximum reliance
>5% to 10%	moderate reliance
>10%	no reliance (e.g. no compliance testing, maximum substantive testing)

compliance tested one error is found. The auditor wants to be 90 per cent confident.

Rearranging the attribute-sampling formula – sample size = reliability factor / UEL – for attribute sampling for compliance testing (see Chapter 5) we get:

$$UEL = \text{reliability factor} / \text{sample size}$$

The reliability factor for one error at 90 per cent confidence is 3.89 (from Table 4.1)

$$UEL = 3.89 / 50 = 7.8\%, \text{ i.e. moderate reliance}$$

In the next sample compliance tested no errors are found:

$$UEL = 2.31 / 50 = 4.6\%, \text{ maximum reliance}$$

The next compliance test two errors are found:

$$UEL = 5.33 / 50 = 10.7\%, \text{ just unacceptable!}$$

And so on. By now it is clear that for these samples no errors means maximum reliance, one error moderate reliance, two or more errors no reliance. The audit approach that will be taken in each case will, naturally, depend on all the other circumstances. Perhaps the auditor will use the results to decide how much extra compliance evidence to seek, or how much substantive testing to perform on the transactions affected by each control. Perhaps they will:

- rely on analytical review for systems where all controls achieve 5 per cent or lower UEL;
- undertake some extra compliance testing combined with some substantive testing on systems falling between the 5–10 per cent range;
- undertake extended substantive testing for systems over the 10 per cent UEL;
- adopt whatever approach their professional judgment, resources, client requirements and so on indicate.

In the fairly straightforward example above, we have assumed that the auditor does not use a risk model to allocate some of the assurance between different audit sources. This would give a lower reliability factor, making the use of smaller sample sizes more practical. During the later stages of auditing this may become a practical option. For example, if an audit approach relies heavily on analytical review and the auditor decides to allocate a quarter of the reliability factor in each sample to this source, the reliability factor for nil errors at 90 per cent confidence would become $2.31 \times 0.75 = 1.73$, and so on. If the sample size remained at 50, the results would be more tolerant of error: for example, at two errors the UEL would be:

$$5.33 \times 0.75 / 50 = 8\% \text{ (moderate reliance)}$$

Or, if the sample size had been reduced to 38, this would give almost the same result as had previously been obtained with a sample of 50

$$5.33 \times 0.75 / 38 = 10.5\% \text{ (just unacceptable)}$$

Clearly, it is open to auditors to construct tables of sample sizes and UELs that they wish to use for their particular audit clients. If, say, it was the auditor's policy at a particular organization to use varying sample sizes for initial compliance testing before taking assurance from any other audit work, then, depending on resources and judgment of tolerable error, a table along the following lines may be appropriate.

At 90 per cent confidence level, the following sample sizes and numbers of errors would give the UELs in Table 9.2 below (rounded to the nearest whole percentage).

Table 9.2   Estimated upper error limits (UELs) to nearest whole percentage from compliance testing at 90% confidence

No. of errors	0	1	2 ...
Sample size			
10	23	39	53 ...
20	12	19	27 ...
30	08	13	18 ...
40	06	10	13 ...
50	05	08	11 ...
60	04	06	09 ...
and so on ...			

Thus if it was judged appropriate to use a sample size of 40 for compliance testing, then nil error indicates 90 per cent confidence in an UEL of up to 6 per cent, one error up to 10 per cent, two errors up to 13 per cent, and so on.

Perhaps the most important aspect of using this technique is to gain experience under the working situations with which you are faced.

Combined sample size for attribute and MUS

Quite often the sample size for substantive testing using MUS will turn out larger than the size for compliance testing, even in systems where moderate reliance on internal control is planned. In this case there is no point in obtaining two samples, if testing situations enable the auditor to validate both controls and calculations using the same documents. This can often turn out to be the case and add quite substantially to the efficiency of the audit. Similarly, for compliance testing alone, when several controls requiring different sample sizes are evidenced on the same document(s), only a single sample, the largest, is required.

Although this is a fairly straightforward point, it is included in some of the case studies in Appendix 1.

Variables sampling

As a general rule variables sampling is too complex to use economically in most financial audit situations. Where convenient software and sufficient time is available, perhaps a major VFM audit, or where error rates are known to be high, this approach can be efficient. (Of course, it might well be argued that in most situations where error rates are known to be high, sampling is unlikely to be the most efficient use of available resources compared to additional audit and management effort to correct the situation.)

We present below a brief overview and would advise auditors to seek further expert advice before undertaking variables sampling.

Variables sampling seeks to estimate the important variables that describe the population: the average value or size of items, the total value within a range (which is why it is useful if lots of errors are thought to exist), mean error per transaction, and so on. Three basic types of variable sampling which we shall briefly consider are:

- mean per unit;
- ratio estimation;
- difference estimation.

Mean per unit sampling

This can be used when the population consists of many similar value transactions and there is little risk of much variation in the value of errors. Basically, mean per unit sampling seeks to estimate the value of, or value of errors in, the population from the mean value per transaction (unit) of/in the sample. This mean value per unit can be multiplied by the number of units in the population.

If populations do not consist of similar value transactions, one of the two following methods might be suitable.

Ratio estimation

This attempts to project errors found in the sample to give an estimate of their value in the population by assuming the direct relationship:

audited value of sample / book value of sample

The book value of the population is multiplied by this ratio to give the auditor's estimate of the true value of the population. This approach assumes that errors occur in proportion to value – the larger the transaction, the larger the error.

Difference estimation

This assumes that the value of the population errors relates to the number of transactions (items) in the population *and* that they are all of similar size, for example the miscalculation of a fixed entitlement.

Audit estimate of population value = book value + $N(a - b)$.

Where:
  a = audit value of sample
  b = book value of sample
  N = number of items (transactions) in population.

So far these approaches are not unduly complex. The complexity comes when trying to work out confidence levels and precision ranges for the statistical conclusions. Unlike the attribute sampling and MUS approaches the auditor will need to calculate what is called a 'standard deviation' to calculate these parameters. The standard deviation measures the spread of sample values around the mean in terms of the square of their deviation from the mean. In practice it is necessary to make an estimate of the standard deviation in order to calculate the required confidence interval and determine the sample size. (This is because one needs the mean to get to the standard deviation in the first place.) Unfortunately, this practice could lead to the need to resample if the standard deviation has been seriously under- or overestimated.

Key formula
The confidence interval around the mean:

$$\text{From } m - k.s \ / \ \sqrt{n} \text{ to } m + k.s \ / \ \sqrt{n}$$

Where:
- m = sample mean
- k = factor from tables
- n = number of items
- s = standard deviation

The standard deviation is derived by finding the difference between the sample mean and each sample value; squaring the answer each time; finding the total of the squared values; dividing this total by one less than the sample size and finding the square root of the answer. In fact, this procedure will only give the sample standard deviation which will differ slightly from the population standard deviation, though for most practical purposes this will not affect the sample size.

Because of the interdependence and problems of estimation mentioned above, auditors may find it convenient to take the largest sample their time and resources will permit on a particular audit. Provided their results are not affected by unexpected errors or other exceptional conditions, they can calculate the standard deviation and confidence level that arise from this sample (tables are also available) and draw their conclusions accordingly. Purists might say this is putting the cart before the horse, but in practice this may be more cost-effective and still satisfy the requirements for adequate audit evidence, particularly when combined with other sources.

Conclusion

Attribute sampling and monetary unit sampling are by far the most practically useful techniques in most audit situations. However, acceptance sampling as a variant on simple attribute sampling can prove very useful, particularly at the early stages of an audit. Although variables sampling is often thought of as the main form of sampling, in other professions it has proved less useful for auditing than some might have expected. The complexity of variables sampling makes computer application essential in most cases.

10   Final concluding thoughts

This book is written with practising auditors in mind and this is the main reason for the number of case studies. If you are uncertain of the techniques outlined, read through the cases again before going back to the text and try to picture each case as far as possible in terms of your own approach to audit.

How should I introduce statistical sampling to my audit?

There are no perfect solutions to this problem, but one thing is almost certain: if statistical sampling is badly introduced, it can ruin relationships and waste effort both for colleagues and clients. For a newcomer to statistical sampling the following steps are suggested, though they are not presented in strict chronological order. At the risk of sounding a little condescending, some of the points below are aimed at the novice level. But even experienced auditors have been known to lose credibility, because in an unfamiliar development they missed an obvious point.

1 Review the areas of audit testing currently undertaken in respect of the real need for sampling: everything must be justified in terms of objectives and the most efficient and effective form of obtaining audit evidence. Do not introduce statistical sampling merely because you know how. If statistical sampling is viable go on to review:

- sample sizes;
- selection method(s);
- experience of audit staff;
- error levels.

2 Unless you have an urgent reason to introduce MUS, plan to introduce attribute sampling for compliance testing of internal control first: it is usually a lot more straightforward.

3 From your initial review:

- Are any current sample sizes larger than might be feasible on a statistical basis? For example, are you testing a large number of insurance or benefit claims, or a large number of payees on the payroll? These will indicate possible savings.
- Are any current samples so small as to give virtually no assurance, or only insignificant assurance? (Consider the formula on p. 108 and Table 9.2, p. 110.) You will need to consider whether it is worth increasing the sample size or obtaining some other form of audit evidence.

4 It can be tempting to start introducing attribute sampling to those areas where quick savings can be made. In the long run, however, building up confidence is more important than quick savings. Go for the low error, well-understood, populations, where you know there are unlikely to be complications, such as a need to subdivide the population because of different processing systems or to stratify it by time period.

5 Agree parameters in line with your professional judgment. At

this stage some auditors, particularly internal ones, would seek to bring managers on board at least in terms of agreeing MTERs, but this may be best avoided first time round if you feel it would cause any confusion.

6 Calculate sample size, sampling interval and produce list of sample items either manually or using convenient software.

7 Carry out testing as appropriate.

8 Review results of testing and any lessons to be learned.

9 Expand and enlarge your experience, moving gradually from obvious systems to systems that are less so.

10 When starting to introduce MUS, undertake an initial review along the lines of that for attribute sampling.

11 Can you introduce MUS on a manual basis to any expenditure audits? This is becoming increasingly unlikely, but can provide invaluable experience. In any event, it may be worth 'shadowing' the audit software to see if it comes up with the same sample size and extrapolation as on a manual basis. Do not worry too much if there are very slight differences, which are probably due to roundings, but if the results are significantly different it may be worth approaching the vendors about the techniques they use. Not everyone is equally cautious, particularly about extrapolation.

12 Can you target large computerized expenditure-processing systems using suitable software? These tend to be more efficient MUS applications.

13 How easy is it going to be to download the data on to your PC? Most packages are PC-based. You will usually need to select only certain fields to download, usually payee reference and amount.

14 Can you test for completeness of the downloaded population? This might be particularly problematical if a sampling program is written in-house, or where non-audit staff have control over installation, maintenance and upgrade. Completeness tests might include straightforward cross-checking to the creditors, payroll, stores and other records. Usually the number of items downloaded can be reconciled with a particular period.

15 Do you, or another auditor, intend undertaking another test program on the downloaded population? If you feel there is a significant risk relating to any relatively predictable false records, such as duplicate payments, payroll ghosts and so on, which you may need to test separately for these before running the sampling program. Otherwise they stand the same chance of being selected as an identical clerical error: the more pounds, the more chance.

16 If the results are unacceptable how should this be presented? Exceeding an UEL by £0.10 due to one highly tainted error may not receive the same response as a £1 million excess when nil errors were anticipated and 12 occurred!

As a general rule it is more efficient to introduce statistical sampling gradually, even if this means that, temporarily, not all auditors are working to the same standard. Opportunities for combined attribute and MUS samples will usually present themselves fairly early on, and should be considered once MUS has been tried.

Ironically one of the problems auditors can face at the start of statistical sampling is that of choosing such stringent parameters that they end up with sample sizes that are too large to be practical. This is ironic, because it prompts some to abandon statistical sampling 'because the samples are too large' and accept smaller samples (that if taken statistically would relate to far less stringent parameters) and ones that usually give little or no assurance. If you simply take a small convenient sample, you are in effect saying your audit objectives do not require you to form an opinion about the whole balance or system under audit, or that you are content to let the parameters 'choose themselves'. It is difficult to decide which is worse: to recognize that you have in the past chosen a sample size that offered lower assurance (less confidence and more risk or a greater than tolerable error level) than professionally acceptable, or that you may now have to do more testing than in the past. But if *you* do not begin to consider the validity and statistical implications of your sample sizes, who else will? On a brighter note, as became apparent in the later chapters, sample size can often be reduced. Provided you are honest and objective, it will be very difficult for anyone to criticize your sample calculations without suggesting fairly definite (though usually more expensive) changes.

Finally, both statistical sampling and audit risk modelling to which it is often linked, are rapidly developing technical aspects of our profession. For those already undertaking statistical sampling, a growing number, the long-term advantages in terms of efficiency, competitive edge and professional standards are potentially enormous.

Appendices

Appendix 1

Additional case studies

The purpose of this appendix is to provide a convenient set of three short exercises and three longer cases for additional practice and/or for copying or modifying to use when training your own staff. The suggested solutions are all at the end of the appendix rather than as part of each case. The cases sometimes include general discussion points on wider implications as well as computations and follow a more flexible structure than cases in the earlier text.

Short Exercises

Exercise 1   Attribute sampling
A stock system internal control is identified as the signing of stores issue notes by authorized signatories. The auditor knows that a few 'errors' can occur usually because the signing officer does not have full authority for the type of issue, but the number of errors is thought to be very low overall. Given the role of this control within the wider system, other sources of evidence and past audit results, it is felt that the compliance testing of

this control must give assurance that the maximum error rate in the population is 4 per cent or less. No sample errors are allowed for and the auditor wants to be 90 per cent confident of the results of this test.

Consider:

- The sample size.
- What to conclude if no sample errors occur.
- What to do if one (or more) sample errors occur.

Exercise 2   Monetary unit sampling

An external auditor is substantively testing year-end balance sheet creditors of £2 170 299. Materiality for the whole accounts has been set at £740 000. No system work or compliance testing of creditors is available.

At the planning stage of the audit it is decided that testing will require 90 per cent confidence level. Previous year results, the results of internal audit work and of analytical review indicates that error levels are likely to be low and no errors are anticipated from the sample.

Find the sample size, assuming the basic precision is set at the materiality level.

The Audit Manager decides that an overall anticipated error (AE) level for the whole accounts of 12 per cent of materiality should be allowed for on each balance tested and, an estimated PGW of 3/5 of the AE should also be allowed for on nominal ledger and personal ledger balances. Overall, auditors are advised to consider using a basic precision 20 per cent below the materiality level.

Consider: the final sample size.

Exercise 3   Monetary unit sampling

Assume the internal auditor was auditing the same balance as in Exercise 2 to the same parameters. However, this auditor has additional compliance evidence that leads him to conclude he can derive around half the assurance he needs before undertaking any substantive work, if the substantive work turns out to be successful, that is, if no errors are found in the sample.

- Discuss how this might affect the allocation of the reliability factor.

Assume the actual results reveal one error, an overstatement of £1.05 on a payment of £15.50.

- Work through the extrapolation stages.
- Form a conclusion and opinion on the year-end creditors.

Cases

Case study I   Attribute sampling

Robert, Internal Audit Manager for a medium-sized organization, is discussing the planned audit of the payroll system with the Chief Accountant, Sharon.

ROBERT: All our visits over the past three years, since I arrived have proved very reassuring.

SHARON: You've never found anything wrong.

ROBERT: One or two small points on internal control.

SHARON: Tiny points, insignificant really, and all put right immediately. Certainly no errors.

ROBERT: One, I think, last year.

SHARON: Oh? ... How much for?

ROBERT: Uh, eleven pence.

Sharon yawns.

ROBERT: Because we are so confident in the integrity of the payroll system, I'm proposing a new audit-testing regime based on taking statistical samples over the year. We won't be doing a lot of flowcharting and asking questions, though we will expect you to let us know if any system changes, manual or computerized, are planned or if you take on new staff.

SHARON: Your people already do fairly regular testing, surely that's enough.

ROBERT: This work will follow the same audit programme; it's basically the way we select the sample that changes. We will tend to select the larger-value items[1] rather than simply picking a few from each department. So your staff won't see more of us; probably less and less as time goes on and assuming we continue to find no errors.

SHARON: Sounds fine, the less the better – no offence.

ROBERT: None taken. We need your help, though, to assist in determining how many records we need to test. We will decide the basic parameters as they are called, but this involves setting ourselves an upper error rate for control lapses, or an upper error limit in pounds. With regard, first, to the control lapses; how would you feel about a rate of, say, 3 per cent?

SHARON: Sounds a bit high to me, say 1 per cent.

ROBERT: Ok. Though the more stringent this rate, the larger the number we will need to test.

SHARON: Well, perhaps 2 per cent then.

Robert spends some time discussing the way he intends to undertake sampling as Sharon has begun to show an interest in this approach. She decides to stick to the 2 per cent MTER and Robert's other parameters are set out below.

Parameters

Overall confidence level required	95%
Number of errors anticipated	0
Reliability factor (from table)	3
Assurance from other sources	0
Precision (MTER)	2%

Robert uses these parameters in a standard, computer-assisted audit software program and it gives him a sample size of 150 (3 / 0.02).

Robert arranges for the same program to interrogate the downloaded payroll details on his PC. (He only downloads

---

[1] An MUS approach is being used where the larger value items have more chance of selection. MUS is often combined with attribute sampling to save taking two separate samples, one to compliance test the controls and another to substantively test the transactions.

sufficient fields to enable him to identify and select each record, as the payroll runs on the organization's mainframe and the PC on which the audit software runs has a much smaller capacity.)

If Robert had a smaller payroll (or almost unlimited time!) he might have considered extracting the sample manually. An example of how this might be done is given later on.

Robert passes the sample of 150 on to his audit section with instructions for them to carry out their usual programme of compliance tests.

Results

Robert's auditors test the sample gradually over the space of a few weeks so as to cause minimum disruption to the work of the payroll office.

The results are as predicted and no compliance errors are found. Robert is able to report to the Financial Director and the organization's Audit Committee that payroll testing indicates that the system internal control is operating to within agreed parameters and to the standard laid down by the organization's financial regulations.

Robert must be careful how he words such a report, as in fact his confidence level was only 95 per cent, i.e. there is a 5 per cent risk implied that his sample will not reflect the larger population for which errors will be greater than 2 per cent. However the ability to offer quantifiable assurance that one is 95 per cent confident error rates are no greater than 2 per cent is considered most acceptable to many bodies.

Robert uses the phrase:

'I have established that, statistically speaking, there is a high level of confidence that internal controls are operating to agreed standards.'

You will have to tailor the precise wording to suit your own organizations and audit objectives.

Discussion points

Is the type of conclusion Robert forms useful from a corporate governance viewpoint?

Do you think managers would generally want more

explanation of, and perhaps input to, the testing parameters than implied above, or less?

What would have been the implications if Robert's team had found an error, i.e. a lapse in internal control?

What if they had found several errors?

- All related to one control?
- Related to different controls?

We discuss the problems surrounding errors later on.

Case study II   Attribute sampling
Edward is auditing the purchases system at XYZ. He has identified three of the key controls as:

- The authorization of purchase orders by the appropriate budget holder.
- The purchase by the central purchasing officer (not a budget holder) who signs each order to confirm purchase has been satisfactorily completed.
- The use of only official, sequential pre-numbered order forms, in triplicate, undercopies retained by the above two officers.

Parameters
Edward usually plans his audit to be 95 per cent confident that internal control has operated effectively over the past twelve months.

By 'effectively' Edward means that exceptions to the first and second key controls are no more than 1 per cent. However, after discussions with management he considers that the third key control should operate effectively 100 per cent of the time. Given his past experience Edward anticipates nil compliance errors in the first control, but allows for one error in the second.

From tables the reliability factor for nil errors and 95 per cent confidence is 3 and for one error and 95 per cent confidence it is 4.75. This means that for the first control Edward will need to test:

$$\text{Reliability factor} / \text{MTER} = 3.00 / 0.01 = 300$$

and for the second control:

$$4.75 / 0.01 = 475$$

Manual extraction

XYZ is a relatively small organization involved in leisure services and there are in fact only 6 008 purchase orders for the year. They are all filed in number (and thus date) order.

Clearly, as both the first and second controls will be tested by examining the same piece of paper, it may well be efficient in this case to test 475 items to satisfy both (rather than 300 for one and 475 for the other).

Edward divides the population, 6 008, by the sample size, 475, to obtain a sampling interval of 12.6. One cannot test 0.6 of an order, so he will examine every 12th order.

Edward picks a random start up to and including 12. He happens to have random number tables available, but he could have picked the first two digits from, say, a £10 note serial number. The random start was 09.

Edward flicks over the order sheets which are serially numbered in the top right hand corner. The ninth one is number 100 364. He extracts this and compliance tests the first two controls (looking, in effect, for the correct signatures). He counts on another twelve to order number 100 376 and repeats the tests: and so on, to order number 106 372 at the end of the year, extracting and testing each 12th order.

As Edward flicks through the orders, counting as he goes, he is also of course testing the sequential numbering, so satisfying the third control.

Edward allows half a second per sheet flicked over as the count continues and ten seconds to check on the signatures. (He has a list of authorized budget holders and sample signatures. Some are a bit difficult to recognize at first and probably take a minute or two, but as he gets used to them it only takes a few seconds to check most.)

The time for the testing is approximately:

$$6\ 008 \times 1/2 \text{ sec} = 50 \text{ mins}$$

plus
$$475 \times 10 \text{ secs} = 1 \text{ hr, } 19 \text{ mins}$$

say, two hours and nineteen minutes for testing. In fact he also allows himself a cup of coffee, chats for a while to one of the order clerks and has a couple of cigarettes (just to aid his concentration). He takes about two and three quarter hours to complete the whole job.

Results
One compliance error for the second control was, as he anticipated, the only error.

Conclusion
Edward writes up his results and concludes that:

... internal control over the purchase order system has operated to the agreed standards for the period audited ...

He shows the unsigned order to the purchasing officer (Edward has a photocopy for his audit file) who signs it as a correction with that day's date.
  The whole assignment takes about three hours before Edward returns to the main audit office and hands in his working papers for review by the audit manager.

Discussion points
- Is it fair to conclude that the controls have been effective for this (part of the) system?
- What if no errors had been found?
- What if an error had been found relating to the third key control?
- What if an error had been found relating to the first key control?
- What if two or three errors had been found relating to any one of the controls?
- What would Edward have done if the first and second controls had required different documents to be examined?

Case study III   Monetary unit sampling
Bill is auditing the creditors at XYZ. He has the same confidence level as Robert (95 per cent, see previous case study), and on the

basis of past results he does not anticipate any errors as the system appears well-controlled and frequent audit checking has found very few inaccuracies to date. He arranges for the creditor's payments to be downloaded to his PC each week and intends to sample them at various points throughout the year, so he can not tell what the final value of the population will be, though it is usually about £6 000 000.

Bill has discussions with finance managers to ensure that the system is not likely to change and no major expansion or similar development is likely to affect his assumptions. He agrees a materiality or maximum tolerable error level of £50 000, less than 1 per cent; in practice, if his results come anywhere close to this, the managers would be most concerned.

Given his opinion (based on various work done by Robert) that the system controls can be relied upon and his intention to take Robert's compliance testing into account, Bill judges he can allocate the reliability factor of 3.0 (95 per cent confidence for nil error) as follows:

Inherent/detection risk	0.5
Internal control evidence	1.5
MUS testing	1.0

In fact, Bill could have used a risk model to allocate the factor if he had felt this was required, particularly if he wished to repeat this sort of allocation over several balances and to be as consistent as possible. Risk-modelling is not a topic that can be covered in the limited time available, but the recommended further reading includes some coverage of this area.

How can Bill obtain a sample given that he has no accurate population figure?

Bill anticipates an error level in the population of £5 000. This is little more than an educated guess and to be on the safe side he assumes that the total of error, precision and any PGW will come to £45 000, leaving a safety margin, also £5 000, in case he does find some small errors. (The smaller the total of all these amounts, the more cautious he is being and the larger the sample he will have to test.)

Consider the final result if:

- no errors are found;
- there is an overpayment of £0.06 on a payment of £47.56;
- there is the above overpayment plus an underpayment of £17 on £15 000.

Suggested solutions and possible points
Exercise 1
Sample Size = rel. factor for 90% confidence & nil error/precision,
= 2.31 / 0.04 = 57.75 (say, 58 items).

- If no errors: conclude that the above parameters have held. That is, 90 per cent confident that the true error rate in the population is less than or equal to 4 per cent.
- If errors are found:
    First error reduces our confidence level to less than 70 per cent for the above sample size! Or, we could resample with a reliability factor of 3.89 in the above equation, giving 98 items. Or we could reconsider the precision. If more than one error found we would be very unlikely to have any acceptable parameters for the population, in this particular case.

Exercise 2
If basic precision set at materiality level. Sample size = 2 170 299 × 2.31 / 740 000 = 6.7 (say 7).

The audit manager is balancing the components for estimated upper error limit to allow a reasonable gap below materiality to cater for any errors, a safety margin. If they did not consider this a reasonable approach, it is likely that a material level of error would already be suspected and the manager might be thinking of qualifying the audit opinion!

The AE (MLE + B.P.) − 12% of materiality = £88 800 + 3 / 5 for PGW, that is, £53 280 = £142 080. In the absence of any further advice sample size would be:

$$2\ 170\ 299 \times 2.31 / 142\ 080 = 35.29 \text{ (say, 36).}$$

In fact this would be a rather prudent and arguably an inefficient sample size based on total precision well below materiality.
But more general advice to auditors in this organization seems
to be to use a total precision that comes up to 20 per cent below
the level of materiality; 20 per cent of the materiality level is
148 000, this deducted from materiality equals 592 000. This
advice gives a less prudent and more efficient sample size of:

2 170 299 × 2.31 / 592 000 = 8.46 (say 9) (see Worksheet 1).

This case helps to illustrate the wide degree of judgment
required in statistical sampling. In general the more confident
of your own assumptions and judgments you become, the
smaller the sample size you may be prepared to accept.

Exercise 3
The internal auditor might use his judgment or a risk model to
allocate some of the total reliability factor to compliance testing,
reducing the size of the reliability factor used for his MUS substantive tests, perhaps by as much as half.
  See Worksheet 1 for the rest of Exercise 3.

Case Study I
Discussion points   From a corporate governance standpoint this
type of statement and statistical sampling in general can offer
measurable assurance regarding the reliability of internal control. The auditor is helped to achieve a more clearly structured,
defensible and professional approach to underpin their opinion
on the adequacy of internal control.
  The implications of an error in this case would depend on
how strictly the chosen parameters were viewed: one error
might just be acceptable here, or a resample could be worth
undertaking.
  If several errors were found either initially or upon carrying
out further work resulting from a first error, and all these related to one particular control, it might be possible to isolate the
effect of a negative conclusion, depending on the importance of
the control and the feasibility of relying upon compensating

control(s). If several errors relating to different controls were found, the auditor would normally conclude that the system had poor internal control and could not be relied upon and management/further audit action would be recommended. Bear in mind that the auditor would usually be using sampling for systems thought to be acceptable and for sample sizes calculated assuming nil or only one or two errors.

Case Study II

Discussion points   The controls do appear to have been effective, but as usual one must stress that this is for the parameters chosen.

If no errors had been found the conclusion is the same as above.

An error relating to the third key control would be serious, and no reliance could be placed on this control given the initial parameter chosen. Urgent action required – increase testing and steps taken to ensure no repeat.

An error relating to the first key control might be less serious – possible reconsideration of the initial parameter or re-sample.

If more errors are found relating to any of the controls this will almost certainly call into question the overall reliability of the system, especially if spread over different controls.

If different documents are needed to be examined, two samples would have been taken, 300 and 475.

Additional Points   How many controls might be distinguished in this case?

Several control implications may arise from one action or arrangement – e.g. the use of forms.

Case Study III

Bill can obtain a sample using the formula:

$$\text{Sample interval} = \text{precision} / \text{reliability factor,}$$

in this case 50 000 and so he would 'hit' every 50 000th pound.

See Worksheet 2 for the final results of this case. The final conclusion should be based on an upper error limit of just over

£45 000, and no real likelihood that a material error could arise from the creditor's figures, given the parameters chosen.

OVER/UNDERSTATEMENTS* COMBINED EVALUATION SHEET

Error No.	A Recorded Value £	B Audited Value £	C Over/Under-statement Errors (A − B)	D Tainting % (C/A)	E Ranking (Highest First)	F Sampling Interval	G Projectal Error £ (D × F)
1	15.50	14.45	1.05	1.05 15.50 = 0.0677 = 6.77%	First	POPULATION [SAMPLE SIZE] 2,170,299 9 = 241,144.33 ie 241,144 [THIS ASSUMES AUDITOR FOLLOWS THROUGH TO ADVICE ON PAGE 124]	16325.45

NOTES:
* Delete as appropriate and use separate sheets for over and understatements.
** This column can be ignored if nil errors were anticipated and the book value of population was accurately known at the planning stage.
Column 1 can then be taken simply as the basic precision chosen.
(If the final UEL is just over materiality check that the value of column I would not have been reduced by using columns H × F where column F was calculated without rounding up.)
*** This can be calculated using the formula. PGW Factor = (reliability factor for current error − reliability factor for previous + nil errors) − 1.

$$3.89 \quad - \quad 2.31 \quad -1 \quad = \quad 0.58$$

Worksheet 1

H** Reliability Factor for Nil Errors	I Basic Precision £ (F × H)	J*** PGW Factor (from tables)	K PGW £ (D × F × J)	L 'Key' Item Errors £	M Most Likely Error (MLE) £ (G + L)	N Upper Error Limit (UEL) £ (I + K + M)	Comments
2.31 [90% confid level and nil errors] [*NOTE* IF COMPLIANCE EVIDENCE WERE TO BE TAKEN INTO ACCOUNT AT THIS STAGE, THIS FACTOR COULD BE REDUCED]	241,144 × 2.31 = 557,042.64 [*NOTE* THIS IS LESS THAN THE 592,000 ADVISED (P133) BECAUSE OF ROUNDING UP FROM 8.46 TO 9 AND DOWN FROM 241,144.33 TO 241,144(F).]	0.58 [see below for manual calculation]	ie G × J 16,325.45 × 0.58 = 9,468.76	N/A in this example. THESE ARE LARGE ITEMS – LARGER THAN THE SAMPLING- INTERVAL – TAKEN OUT TO BE TESTED SEPARATELY. DO NOT MAKE ANY SPECIAL EFFORT TO IDENTIFY THESE AS THE SAMPLE WILL INCLUDE THEM ANYWAY.	16,325.45	557,042 (Basic Precision) + 9,469 (PGW) + 16,325 (MLE) = 582,836	THIS IS WELL BELOW THE MATERIALITY LEVEL.

N.B. When drafting a final conclusion the auditor must remember to:-

i)　Add or deduct the net value of the errors discovered (C + L) from the value of the final population.

ii)　Deduct overstatement errors from the value of the UEL for overstatements and understatement errors from the UEL for understatement in columns C and N).

iii)　Include in the wording of the conclusion the net MLF (M) as the point estimate, the chosen confidence level and the UELs (N) as the range of precision.

OVER/UNDERSTATEMENTS* COMBINED EVALUATION SHEET

Error No.	A Recorded Value £	B Audited Value £	C Over/Under-statement Errors (A − B)	D Tainting % (C/A)	E Ranking (Highest First)	F Sampling Interval	G Projectal Error £ (D × F)
1	47.56	47.50	0.06	0.06 / 47.56 = 0.126%	1st of the overs	45,000	.126% × 45,000 = 56.70
1	15,000	15,017	17	17 / 15,000 = 0.113%	1st of the unders	45,000	50.85

NOTES:
* Delete as appropriate and use separate sheets for over- and understatements.
** This column can be ignored if nil errors were anticipated and the book value of population was accurately known at the planning stage.
Column 1 can then be taken simply as the basic precision chosen.
(If the final UEL is just over materiality check that the value of column I would not have been reduced by using columns H × F where column F was calculated without rounding up.)
*** This can be calculated using the formula. PGW Factor = (reliability factor for current error − reliability factor for previous at nil errors) − 1.

Worksheet 2   (Note: overs and unders should be evaluated separately)

H** Reliability Factor for Nil Errors	I Basic Precision £ (F × H)	J*** PGW Factor (from tables)	K PGW £ (D × F × J)	L 'Key' Item Errors £	M Most Likely Error (MLE) £ (G + L)	N Upper Error Limit (UEL) £ (I + K + M)	Comments
1.0	45,000	0.58	G × J 0.126% × 45,000 × 0.58 = 32.89	N/A	56.70	45,000 + 32.89 + 56.70 45,089.59	Well below Materiality
1.0	45,000	0.58	0.113% × 45,000 × 0.58 = 29.49	N/A	50.85	45,000 + 29.49 + 50.85 45,080.34	"

N.B. When drafting a final conclusion the auditor must remember to:-
i)   Add or deduct the net value of the errors discovered (C + L) from the value of the final population.
ii) Deduct overstatement errors from the value of the UEL for overstatement and understatement errors from the UEL for understatements (columns C and N).
iii) Include in the wording of the conclusion the net MLE (M) as the point estimate, the chosen confidence level and the UELs (N) as the range of precision.

NOTE RE COLUMN E
IF MORE THAN ONE ERROR OCCURS THESE ARE RANKED BY VALUE, THE LARGEST FIRST (STILL KEEP OVERS AND UNDERS SEPARATE). THIS ENSURES THE LARGEST ERRORS GET THE MOST EXTRAPOLATION

Appendix 2

Glossary

Note that these terms are chosen with an audit situation in mind to provide a brief practical understanding rather than a 'watertight' statistical definition applicable to any possible scenario. Not all the terms chosen are ones used in this book.

Acceptance sampling   The acceptance or rejection of a population depending on the number of errors found in an attribute sample (see below).

Attribute sampling   A form of sampling that tests for the presence or absence of an attribute in each item and estimates the extent of this characteristic in the population. A simple yes/no situation such as the presence or absence of a signed authorization.

Audit risk   See **Risk**

Basic precision   The initial range uncertainty associated with sampling results depending on the confidence level (see below) and sample size used. The basic precision may need to be adjusted in the light of the results. The product of the sample size and basic precision (measured as a proportion of the population, is sometimes called the basic precision constant or **basic precision factor**.

141

Bias   Allowing conscious or unconscious preference to affect the items chosen in a sampling context. See also **Random**.

Block sample   A sample that picks a 'block' of items, usually according to a time period, for example, a week's transactions from a year.

Central limit theorem   Implies that if a large number of samples are drawn from a population the sample means are distributed in a bell shaped curve called a *normal curve*, almost irrespective of the original shape of the population distribution. This underlies much of statistical sampling theory.

Cluster sampling   A sampling approach that divides the population into groups or clusters usually on the basis of fairly obvious groupings inherent in the way the population is ordered, for example, on a regional or spatial basis, and samples each cluster.

Compliance tests   Tests of the effective operation of internal control, also used in the context of regulatory compliance. Compare to **Substantive Tests**.

Confidence   A probability in percentage terms about the population value or characteristic being estimated. The *confidence interval* is used to describe a range of values within which such a population quantity lies. For example, to be 90 per cent confident (the confidence level) that an estimate of £x error lies within the range from £x − 30 to £x + 30 (the confidence interval).

Deviation   Usually a failure to comply with or operate an internal control.

Difference estimation   A type of variables sampling (see Chapter 9).

Discovery sampling   A variant of acceptance sampling (see above) that usually involves sampling to the first discovered error.

Fixed interval selection   Sample items are selected at equal intervals throughout the population, that is, at a *sampling interval* equal to the population/sample size.

Haphazard sampling An approach to sampling (see Chapter 2) involving attempts to minimize conscious bias, but without any formal statistical or equivalent audit plan.

Interval sampling See **Fixed interval selection** and **Confidence interval**.

Judgmental sampling An approach to sampling (see Chapter 2) involving non-statistical methods of arriving at the sample size and any inferences from the results. Most *non-statistical sampling* in effect involves some elements of the judgmental approach.

Materiality In audit terms: the amount of error that could be tolerated in a set of accounts, or the tolerable level of errors generally, before the auditor is forced to consider significant action such as qualifying an audit report or requiring significant management action. Sometimes equated to the *maximum tolerable error level* (MTEL). See also **Upper error level**.

Mean An average: the sum of a number of values divided by the number. Used in the *mean per unit* approach to variables sampling (see Chapter 9).

Median The mid-point value of a range or population.

Mode The most frequently occurring value of a range or population.

Monetary unit sampling A statistical sampling approach that uses individual £s, $s, etc. as the monetary sampling units (see Chapter 6).

Most likely error A point (value or rate) sample estimate of the error level in the population.

Net most likely error The net value of the most likely errors of over- and underpayments (see also **Most likely error**). One of the possible stages arrived at when extrapolating monetary errors found from a sample.

Non-sampling-error   Error arising from causes other than any inherent in the use of a sample, for example, poor recording of results. Contrast with **Sampling error** inherent in the risk that a sample is not representative of the population.

Non-statistical sampling   See **Judgmental sampling**.

Normal curve   See **Central limit theorem**.

Normal distribution   The bell shape of the data plotted when attempting to show the normal curve.

Point estimate   The estimated value or rate of error, control deviation, etc. in the population, arrived at from the sample results (usually stated subject to a confidence level and precision in statistical evaluations).

Population   The whole set of items, control events, etc. to be sampled.

Population characteristic   Whatever aspect of the population is to be estimated from taking a sample, e.g. the rate of internal control deviation.

Precision   The range or confidence interval (see above) in which a point estimate is said to lie (see also **Basic precision**).

Precision gap widening   An adjustment to basic precision (see above) to take account of more than anticipated errors.

Probability proportional to size   The name given to sampling approaches that enable the likelihood of items being selected to depend on the size of those items, by choosing the common units making up the items as the sampling units. Thus, the likelihood of invoices being selected will depend on their value, i.e. the number of pounds they contain. See also **Monetary unit sampling**.

Probability theory   A complex accumulation of logical and mathematical reasoning underlying the use of statistical sampling that enables an estimation of the likelihood of outcomes, from nil to certainty.

Random sample   A sample where bias is avoided by ensuring that every item in the population has an equal or known chance of selection.

Ratio estimate   A type of variables sampling (see Chapter 9).

Reliability factor   A measure of the assurance associated with the basic precision, obtained in practice from the confidence level and anticipated number of errors (see p. 33).

Sampling error   See **Non-sampling error**.

Sampling frame   A convenient list of items from which the sample is drawn.

Sampling unit   Individual items in the sampling frame some of which will be selected as the sample.

Sampling with replacement   Items sampled are 'replaced' in the population and might be selected again. Sampling *without replacement*, of course, ensures that items selected are not replaced.

Skewness   The 'lopsidedness' or asymmetrical nature of a distribution. Most accounting distributions are skewed, often more to the left. Compare to the **Normal distribution**.

Standard deviation   A summary of the squares of the deviations of a set of values about their mean.

Statistical sampling   A basic approach to sampling (see Chapter 2) in accordance with probability theory.

Stratified sampling   A sampling approach that divides the population into different levels or strata usually on the basis of value and samples separately from each stratum.

Substantive tests   Testing to substantiate the detail of items, for example, the completeness, accuracy and validity of transactions. Compare to **Compliance tests**.

Systematic sampling   Effectively this is interval sampling with a random start.

Tainting   The proportion: error/book value, used for example when extrapolating MUS errors.

t-distribution   An alternative to the normal distribution (see above) used when dealing with smaller populations and sample sizes than required for the normal distribution. Its mathematical properties are different from the normal distribution.

Upper error level (UEL)   The upper end of the precision range (see above), useful for stating the estimate of maximum error in a population arising from sampling results and then comparing to the MTEL or materiality.

Variables sampling   A statistical sampling approach that estimates key variables of a population such as its mean (see Chapter 9).

Appendix 3

Abbreviations

Although most readers/auditors will recognize and take these abbreviations for granted the following are presented for the sake of convenience. The possible range of technical abbreviations has been limited to those used in this book and explained in the text.

Organizational

ACCA   Association of chartered certified accountants
AICPA   American institute of certified public accountants
APB   Auditing practices board (a board of the CCAB: see below)
APC   Auditing practices committee (forerunner of ABP)
CCAB   Consultative committee of accounting bodies
CIMA   Chartered institute of management accountants
CIPFA   Chartered institute of public finance and accountancy
IAPC   International audit practices committee (of the IFA)
ICAEW   Institute of chartered accountants in England and Wales

IFA	International federation of accountants
IIA	Institute of internal auditors
IMTA	Institute of municipal treasurers and accountants (now CIPFA)

Technical

AE	Anticipated error
AR	Analytical review and/or audit risk (dual use)
BP	Basic precision
CR	Control risk
DR	Detection risk
CT	Compliance testing (of internal control)
DST	Direct substantive testing
IR	Inherent risk
MTEL	Maximum tolerable error level (usually in money terms)
MTER	Maximum tolerable error rate (usually in percentages)
MUS	Monetary unit sampling
PGW	Precision gap widening
PPS	Probability proportional to size
RF	Reliability factor (Rel. Fac.)
SAS	Statement of auditing standards (issued by the APB, see above)
SBA	Systems based audit/approach
UEL	Upper error level
VFM	Value for money

Appendix 4

SAS 430

The following pages are reproduced with permission of the Auditing Practices Board from SAS 430 Audit Sampling.

STATEMENT OF AUDITING STANDARDS

430 – AUDIT SAMPLING

Statements of Auditing Standards ('SASs') are to be read in the light of 'The scope and authority of APB pronouncements'. In particular, they contain basic principles and essential procedures ('Auditing Standards'), indicated by paragraphs in bold type, with which auditors are required to comply in the conduct of any audit. SASs also include explanatory and other material which is designed to assist auditors in interpreting and applying Auditing Standards. The definitions in the Glossary of terms are to be applied in the interpretation of SASs.

Introduction
1 The purpose of this SAS is to set standards and provide guidance on the design and selection of an audit sample

and the evaluation of the sample results. This SAS applies equally to both statistical and non-statistical sampling methods. It applies to any audit using sampling whether related to financial statements or not. Nothing contained in this statement is intended to preclude non-statistically based samples where there are reasonable grounds for believing that the results may be relied on for the purpose of the test.

2   When using either statistical or non-statistical sampling methods, auditors should design and select an audit sample, perform audit procedures thereon and evaluate sample results so as to obtain appropriate audit evidence. (SAS 430.1)

3   In forming their audit opinion, auditors do not normally examine all of the information available. It is generally impractical to do so and valid conclusions can be reached using audit sampling.

4   'Audit sampling' means the application of audit procedures to less than 100% of the items within an account balance or class of transactions to enable auditors to obtain and evaluate audit evidence about some characteristic of the items selected in order to form or assist in forming a conclusion concerning the population which makes up the account balance or class of transactions.

5   It is important to recognise that certain testing procedures do not come within the definition of sampling. Tests performed on 100% of the items within a population do not involve sampling. Likewise applying audit procedures to all items within a population which have a particular characteristic (for example all items over a certain amount) does not qualify as audit sampling with respect to the portion of the population examined, nor with regard to the population as a whole, since the items were not selected from the total population on a basis that was expected to be representative.

6   Statistically based sampling involves the use of techniques from which mathematically constructed conclusions about the population can be drawn. Auditors draw a judg-

mental opinion about the population from non-statistical methods.

Design of the sample

7 When designing the size and structure of an audit sample, auditors should consider the specific audit objectives, the nature of the population from which they wish to sample, and the sampling and selection methods. (SAS 430.2)

Audit objectives

8 Auditors first consider the specific audit objectives to be achieved and the audit procedures which are most likely to achieve those objectives. In addition, when audit sampling is appropriate, consideration of the nature of the audit evidence sought and possible error conditions or other characteristics relating to that evidence assists auditors in defining what constitutes an error and what population to use for sampling. For example, when performing tests of control over an entity's purchasing procedures, auditors may be concerned with matters such as whether an invoice was clerically checked and properly approved. On the other hand, when performing substantive procedures on invoices processed during the period, auditors are concerned with matters such as the proper reflection of the amounts payable and of the monetary amounts of such invoices in the financial statements.

Population

9 The population is the entire set of data from which auditors wish to sample in order to reach a conclusion. Therefore the population from which the sample is drawn has to be appropriate and complete for the specific audit objective. For example, if the auditors' objective is to test for overstatement of debtors, the population may be defined as the debtors listing. On the other hand, when testing for understatement of creditors, the population is not the creditors listing but rather subsequent disbursements, unpaid

invoices, suppliers' statements, unmatched goods received notes or other populations that can provide evidence of understatement of creditors.

10   The individual items that make up the population may be described as sampling units. The population can be divided into sampling units in a variety of ways. For example, if the auditors' objective is to test the validity of debtors, the sampling unit may be defined as customer balances or individual customer invoices. In monetary unit sampling each £1 of, for example, a debtors balance listing is the sampling unit. Auditors define the sampling unit in order to obtain an efficient and effective sample to achieve the particular audit objectives.

11   To assist in the efficient and effective design of the sample, stratification may be appropriate. Stratification is the process of dividing a population into sub-populations, each of which is a group of sampling units, which have similar characteristics (often monetary value). The strata are explicitly defined so that each sampling unit can belong to only one stratum. This process can be used to reduce the variability of the items within each stratum. Stratification therefore enables auditors to direct audit effort towards the items which, for example, contain the greatest potential monetary error. For example, they may direct attention to larger value items for debtors to detect material overstatement errors.

Sample size

12   When determining sample sizes, auditors should consider sampling risk, the amount of error that would be acceptable and the extent to which they expect to find errors. (SAS 430.3)

13   Examples of some factors affecting sample size are contained in the Appendix.

Sampling risk

14   Sampling risk arises from the possibility that the auditors' conclusion, based on a sample, may be different from the

conclusion that would be reached if the entire population were subjected to the same audit procedure.[1]

15 Auditors are faced with sampling risk in both tests of control and substantive procedures as follows:

(a) tests of control

(i) the risk of placing a higher than necessary assessment on control risk, because the error in the sample is greater than the error in the total population; or

(ii) the risk of placing a lower than required assessment on control risk, because the error in the sample is less than the error in the population as a whole.

(b) substantive tests

(i) the risk of concluding that a recorded account balance or class of transactions is materially misstated when it is not, because the error in the sample is greater than the error in the population as a whole; or

(ii) the risk of concluding that a recorded account balance or class of transactions is acceptable when it is materially misstated, because the error in the sample is less than the error in the population as a whole.

16 Sample size is affected by the degree of sampling risk that auditors are willing to accept from the results of the sample, which depends upon the importance of the results of the audit procedure involving sampling to the auditors' conclusions. The greater their reliance on the results, the lower the sampling risk auditors are willing to accept and the larger the sample size needs to be. Auditors consider

---

[1] Sampling risk can be contrasted with non-sampling risk which arises when auditors use any audit procedures. Non-sampling risk arises because, for example, most audit evidence is persuasive rather than conclusive, or auditors might use inappropriate procedures or might misinterpret evidence and thus fail to recognise an error. Auditors attempt to reduce non-sampling risk to a negligible level by appropriate planning, direction, supervision and review.

sample size in the context of the overall risk assessment (see SAS 300 'Accounting and internal control systems and audit risk assessments').

Tolerable error

17   Tolerable error is the maximum error in the population that auditors are willing to accept and still conclude that the audit objective has been achieved. Tolerable error is considered during the planning stage and, for substantive procedures, is related to the auditors' judgment about materiality. The smaller the tolerable error, the larger is the sample size as a proportion of the population.

18   In tests of control, the tolerable error is the maximum rate of deviation from a prescribed control procedure that auditors are willing to accept in the population and still conclude that the preliminary assessment of control risk is valid. In substantive procedures, the tolerable error is the maximum monetary error in an account balance or class of transactions that auditors are willing to accept so that, when the results of all audit procedures are considered, they are able to conclude, with reasonable assurance, that the financial statements are not materially misstated.

Expected error

19   If auditors expect error to be present in the population, a larger sample than when no error is expected generally has to be examined to conclude that the actual error in the population is not greater than the planned tolerable error. The size and frequency of errors is important in assessing the sample size. Larger sample sizes arise, for the same overall error, if there are a few large errors compared to where there are many small ones. Smaller sample sizes result when the population is expected to be error free. If the expected error rate is high then sampling may not be appropriate. In determining the expected error in a population, auditors consider such matters as the size and frequency of errors identified in previous audits, changes in the entity's procedures and evidence available from other procedures.

Selection of the sample

20 Auditors should select sample items in such a way that the sample can be expected to be representative of the population in respect of the characteristics being tested. (SAS 430.4)

21 For a sample to be representative of the population, all items in the population are required to have an equal or known probability of being selected.

22 While there are a number of selection methods, three methods commonly used are:

- random selection, which ensures that all items in the population have an equal chance of selection, for example by use of random number tables;
- systematic selection, which involves selecting items using a constant interval between selections, the first interval having a random start. When using systematic selection, auditors ensure that the population is not structured in such a manner that the sampling interval corresponds with a particular pattern in the population; and
- haphazard selection, which may be an acceptable alternative to random selection provided auditors are satisfied that the sample is representative of the entire population. This method requires care to guard against making a selection which is biased, for example towards items which are easily located, as they may not be representative.

Evaluation of sample results

23 Having carried out, on each sample item, those audit procedures which are appropriate to the particular audit objective, auditors should:

(a) analyse any errors detected in the sample; and

(b) draw inferences for the population as a whole. (SAS 430.5)

Analysis of errors in the sample

24 In analysing the errors detected in the sample, auditors first determine that an item in question is in fact an error. In

designing the sample, auditors define those conditions which constitute an error by reference to the audit objectives. For example, in a substantive procedure relating to the recording of debtors, a misposting between customer accounts does not affect the total debtors. Therefore, it may be inappropriate to consider this an error in evaluating the sample results of this particular procedure, even though it may have an effect on other areas of the audit such as the assessment of doubtful debts.

25   When the expected audit evidence regarding a specific sample item cannot be obtained, auditors may be able to obtain sufficient appropriate audit evidence through performing alternative procedures. For example, if a positive debtors confirmation has been requested but no reply received, auditors may be able to obtain sufficient appropriate audit evidence of the debt by reviewing subsequent payments from the customer. If they are able to perform satisfactory alternative procedures, the item is not treated as an error.

26   Auditors also consider the qualitative aspects of the errors. These include the nature and cause of the error and the possible effect of the error on other phases of the audit.

27   In analysing the errors discovered, auditors may observe that many have a common feature, for example type of transaction, location, product line or period of time. In such circumstances, they may decide to identify all items in the population which possess the common feature, thereby producing a sub-population, and extend audit procedures in this area. They may then perform a separate analysis based on the items examined for each sub-population, so that they have sufficient appropriate audit evidence for each sub-population.

Inferences to be drawn from the population as a whole

28   Auditors project the error results of the sample to the population from which the sample was selected, ensuring that the method of projection is consistent with the method used to select the sampling unit. The projection of the

sample involves estimating the probable error in the population (by extrapolating the errors found in the sample), and estimating any further error that might not have been detected because of the imprecision of the technique. This is in addition to the consideration of the qualitative aspects of any errors found.

29   Auditors consider whether errors in the population might exceed the tolerable error. To accomplish this, they compare the projected population error to the tolerable error taking into account the results of other audit procedures relevant to the specific control or financial statement assertion. The projected population error used for this comparison in the case of substantive procedures is net of adjustments made by the entity. When the projected population error exceeds the tolerable error, they re-assess the sampling risk and, if that risk is unacceptable, consider extending the audit procedure or performing alternative audit procedures, either of which may result in them proposing an adjustment to the financial statements.

Compliance with International Standards on Auditing

30   Compliance with this SAS ensures compliance in all material respects with International Standard on Auditing 530 'Audit Sampling'.

Effective date

31   Auditors are required to comply with the Auditing Standards contained in this SAS in respect of audits of financial statements for periods ending on or after 23 December 1995.

THE AUDITING
PRACTICES BOARD

SOME FACTORS INFLUENCING SAMPLE SIZE

SAS 430.3 states that 'when determining sample sizes, auditors should consider sampling risk, the amount of error that would be acceptable and the extent to which they expect to find errors'. Factors affecting sample size are set out in the tables below.

The Auditing Standards and guidance included in SAS 220 'Audit materiality', SAS 300 'Accounting and internal control systems and audit risk assessments' and SAS 400 'Audit evidence' are also relevant when using these tables.

Table 1 – Some factors influencing sample size for tests of controls

Factor	Impact on sample size
Sampling risk	• The greater the reliance on the results of a test of control using audit sampling, the lower the sampling risk auditors are willing to accept and, consequently, the larger the sample size. • The lower the assessment of control risk, the more likely auditors are to place reliance on audit evidence from tests of control. • A high control risk assessment may result in a decision not to perform tests of control.
Tolerable error rate	The higher the tolerable rate the lower the sample size and vice versa.
Expected error rate	• If errors are expected, a larger sample usually needs to be examined to confirm that the actual error rate is less than the tolerable error rate. • High expected error rates may result in a decision not to perform tests of control.
Number of items in population	Virtually no effect on a sample size unless population is small.

Table 2 – Some factors influencing sample size for substantive tests

Factor	Impact on sample size
Inherent risk[1]	• The higher the assessment of inherent risk, the more audit evidence is required to support the auditors' conclusion.
Control risk[2]	• The higher the assessment of control risk, the greater the reliance on audit evidence obtained from substantive procedures. • A high control risk assessment may result in the decision not to perform tests of control and reliance entirely on substantive procedures.
Detection risk[3]	• Sampling risk for substantive tests is one form of detection risk. The lower the sampling risk auditors are willing to accept, the larger the sample size. • Other substantive procedures may provide audit evidence regarding the same financial statement assertions and reduce detection risk. This may reduce the extent of the auditors' reliance on the results of a substantive procedure using audit sampling. • The lower the reliance on the results of a substantive procedure using audit sampling, the higher the sampling risk auditors are willing to accept and, consequently, the smaller the sample size.
Tolerable error rate	The higher the monetary value of the tolerable error the smaller the sample size and vice versa.
Expected error rate	If errors are expected, a larger sample usually needs to be examined to confirm that the actual error rate is less than the tolerable error rate.
Population value	The less material the monetary value of the population to the financial statements, the smaller the sample size that may be required.
Numbers of items in population	Virtually no effect on sample size unless population is small.
Stratification	If it is appropriate to stratify the population this may redirect the sample and lead to a smaller sample size.

1   *Inherent risk is the susceptibility of an account balance or class of transactions to material misstatement, either individually or when aggregated with misstatements in other balances or classes, irrespective of related internal controls.*

2   *Control risk is the risk that a misstatement that could occur in an account balance or class of transactions and that could be material, either individually or when aggregated with misstatements in other balances or classes, would not be prevented, or detected and corrected on a timely basis, by the accounting and internal control systems.*

3   *Detection risk is the risk that auditors' substantive procedures do not detect a misstatement that exists in an account balance or class of transactions that could be material, either individually or when aggregated with misstatements in other balances or classes.*

Appendix 5

Tables

The only tables included in this appendix are those related directly to matters dealt with in the main text. If you need to use statistical tables to any significant extent, many excellent collections are currently published and are well worth the small price usually charged.

Table 1, the random numbers table, has been generated using a standard computer program – one of many easily available. To use Table 1, first decide the range of numbers from which you wish to select and how many numbers you want: for example, 'from a population numbered 50 to 5 000 inclusive I wish to select ten random numbers'. Then starting at any point (most people start at the top left and read down, but you can start in the middle and read across or at the bottom and read up, as you wish) read off consecutive groups of as many digits as in the upper limit of your range (four in this case). Ignoring any values outside the range, keep going in the same direction until you have as many (ten in this case) as you want. Most longer random number tables in specialized statistical publications collect the digits into convenient blocks to make them easier to read.

Table 2 shows the cumulative poisson probabilities from

which individual reliability factors can be inferred, for example, the nearest reliability factor (corresponding to the *m* value) for a 95 per cent confidence level, no errors, is 3.0; 99 per cent is 4.6 and so on.

Table 1   Random numbers

6789	3095	9848	8271	9973		6269	8269	6925	6071	6138
1423	5617	0895	0224	7712		0834	3702	7229	6083	9618
1122	7607	5459	0607	7322		4152	5325	0538	8180	3542
3920	9291	9003	3982	0165		6487	3231	6942	1196	2372
3963	4636	1503	4047	7362		4364	7207	5471	7462	3440
6636	5653	9862	8023	5539		6714	8286	8386	7958	4019
3053	5249	5895	0083	2695		5034	5810	5964	4713	3643
0275	9681	7728	5032	9883		0671	3956	8493	8830	9807
4126	5153	7997	1307	2176		1459	4940	7638	3260	6740
7440	9914	2721	5417	2406		3830	2432	7765	2617	6337
3712	9831	7400	5573	7517		3506	4269	5545	6091	2428
3318	7932	0780	6401	2818		1982	4088	0044	3713	8074
3852	1892	8712	2694	0629		6083	8041	8705	0605	7137
9756	3296	4277	0504	5718		1919	7936	3115	9397	6530
2962	5239	0796	9964	0609		8088	8839	9779	5114	6152
4771	2239	5987	4754	4506		3325	1066	4240	8453	4184
1024	0495	6363	6695	8607		1256	5488	4986	4916	8393
7207	2334	5237	2230	3230		7567	8372	6997	0933	7783
3922	3885	3352	9046	7695		6555	6287	0732	3092	3863
0923	3721	5184	3014	1237		6240	4323	3266	2755	0790
6647	8564	6004	8260	9643		3830	4918	5141	5419	2533
8131	8240	3476	5023	7708		5943	1111	2282	9692	6275
2302	3197	7805	4011	1661		4703	5181	0216	2711	2749
9153	0905	1434	2440	9010		6339	8072	2661	0475	3938
8432	6630	6653	9216	7981		1861	3920	9310	5051	9777
1526	1128	2137	3156	7243		1758	6421	3194	2993	5695
9412	3907	6262	4983	9323		6730	0582	4866	9714	4822
4308	9765	9848	1418	4289		1662	0622	0331	8878	7830
						4229	5818	8182	7548	4365
						3269	0881	3031	3957	1003
						9856	5544	7335	8363	7950

Table 2 Cumulative poisson probabilities

The table gives the probability that r or more random events are contained in an interval when the average number of such events per interval is m, i.e.

$$\sum_{x=r}^{\infty} e^{-m} \frac{m^x}{x!}$$

Where there is no entry for a particular pair of values of r and m, this indicates that the appropriate probability is less than 0.000 05. Similarly, except for the case $r = 0$ when the entry is exact, a tabulated value of 1.0000 represents a probability greater than 0.999 95.

$m =$	0.1	0.2	0.3	0.4	0.5	0.6	0.7	0.8	0.9	1.0
$r = 0$	1.0000	1.0000	1.0000	1.0000	1.0000	1.0000	1.0000	1.0000	1.0000	1.0000
1	.0952	.1813	.2592	.3297	.3935	.4512	.5034	.5507	.5934	.6321
2	.0047	.0175	.0369	.0616	.0902	.1219	.1558	.1912	.2275	.2642
3	.0002	.0011	.0036	.0079	.0144	.0231	.0341	.0474	.0629	.0803
4		.0001	.0003	.0008	.0018	.0034	.0058	.0091	.0135	.0190
5				.0001	.0002	.0004	.0008	.0014	.0023	.0037
6							.0001	.0002	.0003	.0006
7										.0001

$m =$	1.1	1.2	1.3	1.4	1.5	1.6	1.7	1.8	1.9	2.0
$r = 0$	1.0000	1.0000	1.0000	1.0000	1.0000	1.0000	1.0000	1.0000	1.0000	1.0000
1	.6671	.6988	.7275	.7534	.7769	.7981	.8173	.8347	.8504	.8647
2	.3010	.3374	.3732	.4082	.4422	.4751	.5068	.5372	.5663	.5940
3	.0996	.1205	.1429	.1665	.1912	.2166	.2428	.2694	.2963	.3233
4	.0257	.0338	.0431	.0537	.0656	.0788	.0932	.1087	.1253	.1429
5	.0054	.0077	.0107	.0143	.0186	.0237	.0296	.0364	.0441	.0527
6	.0010	.0015	.0022	.0032	.0045	.0060	.0080	.0104	.0132	.0166
7	.0001	.0003	.0004	.0006	.0009	.0013	.0019	.0026	.0034	.0045
8			.0001	.0001	.0002	.0003	.0004	.0006	.0008	.0011
9							.0001	.0001	.0002	.0002

$m =$	2.1	2.2	2.3	2.4	2.5	2.6	2.7	2.8	2.9	3.0
$r = 0$	1.0000	1.0000	1.0000	1.0000	1.0000	1.0000	1.0000	1.0000	1.0000	1.0000
1	.8775	.8892	.8997	.9093	.9179	.9257	.9328	.9392	.9450	.9502
2	.6204	.6454	.6691	.6916	.7127	.7326	.7513	.7689	.7854	.8009
3	.3504	.3773	.4040	.4303	.4562	.4816	.5064	.5305	.5540	.5768
4	.1614	.1806	.2007	.2213	.2424	.2640	.2859	.3081	.3304	.3528
5	.0621	.0725	.0838	.0959	.1088	.1226	.1371	.1523	.1682	.1847
6	.0204	.0249	.0300	.0357	.0420	.0490	.0567	.0651	.0742	.0839
7	.0059	.0075	.0094	.0116	.0142	.0172	.0206	.0244	.0287	.0335
8	.0015	.0020	.0026	.0033	.0042	.0053	.0066	.0081	.0099	.0119
9	.0003	.0005	.0006	.0009	.0011	.0015	.0019	.0024	.0031	.0038
10	.0001	.0001	.0001	.0002	.0003	.0004	.0005	.0007	.0009	.0011
11					.0001	.0001	.0001	.0002	.0002	.0003
12									.0001	.0001

Table 2 Cumulative poisson probabilities – *continued*

m =	3.1	3.2	3.3	3.4	3.5	3.6	3.7	3.8	3.9	4.0
r = 0	1.0000	1.0000	1.0000	1.0000	1.0000	1.0000	1.0000	1.0000	1.0000	1.0000
1	.9550	.9592	.9631	.9666	.9698	.9727	.9753	.9776	.9798	.9817
2	.8153	.8288	.8414	.8532	.8641	.8743	.8838	.8926	.9008	.9084
3	.5988	.6201	.6406	.6603	.6792	.6973	.7146	.7311	.7469	.7619
4	.3752	.3975	.4197	.4416	.4634	.4848	.5058	.5265	.5468	.5665
5	.2018	.2194	.2374	.2558	.2746	.2936	.3128	.3322	.3516	.3712
6	.0943	.1054	.1171	.1295	.1424	.1559	.1699	.1844	.1994	.2149
7	.0388	.0446	.0510	.0579	.0653	.0733	.0818	.0909	.1005	.1107
8	.0142	.0168	.0198	.0231	.0267	.0308	.0352	.0401	.0454	.0511
9	.0047	.0057	.0069	.0083	.0099	.0117	.0137	.0160	.0185	.0214
10	.0014	.0018	.0022	.0027	.0033	.0040	.0048	.0058	.0069	.0081
11	.0004	.0005	.0006	.0008	.0010	.0013	.0016	.0019	.0023	.0028
12	.0001	.0001	.0002	.0002	.0003	.0004	.0005	.0006	.0007	.0009
13				.0001	.0001	.0001	.0001	.0002	.0002	.0003
14									.0001	.0001

m =	4.1	4.2	4.3	4.4	4.5	4.6	4.7	4.8	4.9	5.0
r = 0	1.0000	1.0000	1.0000	1.0000	1.0000	1.0000	1.0000	1.0000	1.0000	1.0000
1	.9834	.9850	.9864	.9877	.9889	.9899	.9909	.9918	.9926	.9933
2	.9155	.9220	.9281	.9337	.9389	.9437	.9482	.9523	.9561	.9596
3	.7762	.7898	.8026	.8149	.8264	.8374	.8477	.8575	.8667	.8753
4	.5858	.6046	.6228	.6406	.6577	.6743	.6903	.7058	.7207	.7350
5	.3907	.4102	.4296	.4488	.4679	.4868	.5054	.5237	.5418	.5595
6	.2307	.2469	.2633	.2801	.2971	.3142	.3316	.3490	.3665	.3840
7	.1214	.1325	.1442	.1564	.1689	.1820	.1954	.2092	.2233	.2378
8	.0573	.0639	.0710	.0786	.0866	.0951	.1040	.1133	.1231	.1334
9	.0245	.0279	.0317	.0358	.0403	.0451	.0503	.0558	.0618	.0681
10	.0095	.0111	.0129	.0149	.0171	.0195	.0222	.0251	.0283	.0318
11	.0034	.0041	.0048	.0057	.0067	.0078	.0090	.0104	.0120	.0137
12	.0011	.0014	.0017	.0020	.0024	.0029	.0034	.0040	.0047	.0055
13	.0003	.0004	.0005	.0007	.0008	.0010	.0012	.0014	.0017	.0020
14	.0001	.0001	.0002	.0002	.0003	.0003	.0004	.0005	.0006	.0007
15				.0001	.0001	.0001	.0001	.0001	.0002	.0002
16									.0001	.0001

m =	5.2	5.4	5.6	5.8	6.0	6.2	6.4	6.6	6.8	7.0
r = 0	1.0000	1.0000	1.0000	1.0000	1.0000	1.0000	1.0000	1.0000	1.0000	1.0000
1	.9945	.9955	.9963	.9970	.9975	.9980	.9983	.9986	.9989	.9991
2	.9658	.9711	.9756	.9794	.9826	.9854	.9877	.9897	.9913	.9927
3	.8912	.9052	.9176	.9285	.9380	.9464	.9537	.9600	.9656	.9704
4	.7619	.7867	.8094	.8300	.8488	.8658	.8811	.8948	.9072	.9182
5	.5939	.6267	.6579	.6873	.7149	.7408	.7649	.7873	.8080	.8270
6	.4191	.4539	.4881	.5217	.5543	.5859	.6163	.6453	.6730	.6993
7	.2676	.2983	.3297	.3616	.3937	.4258	.4577	.4892	.5201	.5503
8	.1551	.1783	.2030	.2290	.2560	.2840	.3127	.3419	.3715	.4013
9	.0819	.0974	.1143	.1328	.1528	.1741	.1967	.2204	.2452	.2709
10	.0397	.0488	.0591	.0708	.0839	.0984	.1142	.1314	.1498	.1695
11	.0177	.0225	.0282	.0349	.0426	.0514	.0614	.0726	.0849	.0985
12	.0073	.0096	.0125	.0160	.0201	.0250	.0307	.0373	.0448	.0534
13	.0028	.0038	.0051	.0068	.0088	.0113	.0143	.0179	.0221	.0270
14	.0010	.0014	.0020	.0027	.0036	.0048	.0063	.0080	.0102	.0128
15	.0003	.0005	.0007	.0010	.0014	.0019	.0026	.0034	.0044	.0057
16	.0001	.0002	.0002	.0004	.0005	.0007	.0010	.0014	.0018	.0024
17		.0001	.0001	.0001	.0002	.0003	.0004	.0005	.0007	.0010
18					.0001	.0001	.0001	.0002	.0003	.0004
19								.0001	.0001	.0001

Source: *Statistical Tables* – 3rd edn by J. Murdoch and J.A. Barnes. Reproduced with kind permission of Macmillan Press Ltd.

Appendix 6

Further reading

This short bibliography is not intended to be comprehensive; rather it offers a selective choice of books that the author feels will help practising auditors to:

- follow up the standards and guidance mentioned in the text; (1)
- gain alternative introductions to audit sampling; (2)
- delve into more advanced treatment of the subject; (3)
- find shorter, summary treatments, useful for training staff. (4)

You are advised to seek whatever is the latest edition, as new editions and reprints are fairly common and older editions are usually out of print.

Author	Title	Publisher	
AICPA (1985),	*SAS 39 Auditing Sampling,*	AICPA	(1)
APB (1995),	*SAS 430 Audit Sampling,*	APB	(1)(2)
APB (1995),	*SAS 300 Accounting and Internal Control Systems and Audit Risk Assessments,*	ABP	(1)

Arkin, H. (1984),	*Handbook of Sampling for Auditing and Accounting,*	McGraw Hill	(2)
Arkin, H. (1984)	*Sampling Methods for the Auditor – an advanced treatment,*	McGraw Hill	(3)
Cadbury Report, the (1992),	*Report of the Committee on the Financial Aspects of Corporate Governance*		
CIPFA (1995),	*Statistics for Audit – a guide to statistical sampling for auditors,*	CIPFA	(3)
Coopers & Lybrand (1995),	*Manual of Auditing* (relevant ch. only),	Gee	(4)
COSO (1992),[1]	*Internal Control – Integrated Framework*		
Guy, D.M., Carmichael, D. and Whittington, O.R. (1984),	*Audit Sampling – an introduction,*	John Wiley	(2)
IFAC (1996),	*International Auditing Guideline No. 19. Audit sampling,*	IFAC	(1)
Jones, P.C. and Bates, J.G. (1994),	*Public Sector Auditing – practical techniques for an integrated approach* (relevant ch. only),	Chapman & Hall	(4)
Leslie, D.A., Teitlebaum, A.D. and Anderson, R.J.	*Dollar Unit Sampling – a practical guide for auditors,*	Pitman Publishing	(3)
MacRae, T.W.	*Statistical Sampling for Audit and Control,*	John Wiley	(3)
Woolf, E. (1986),	*Auditing Today* (relevant ch. only),	Prentice Hall	(4)

---

[1] The Report by the Committee of Sponsoring Organizations of the Treadway Commission.

Index

Acceptance sampling *see* sampling
Accountability 23–5
Attribute sampling *see* sampling
Audit, increasing the value of 19–25

Balances 64–5

Compliance test *see* testing
Confidence 31–3, 61–2, 142
  interval 113
Controls, internal 39–40, 90–93
Corporate governance, implications of
  133

Definitions (glossary) 141–6
Difference estimation 112–14
Download 117

Equal interval selection 13–14
  see also sampling
Errors 36, 59, 155–7
  anticipated 69
  expected 154
  extrapolation under MUS 70–86
  over-payment 75–86
  tolerable 154
  under-payment 82–6

Fixed interval *see* equal interval

Haphazard sampling *see* sampling
Historical context 4

Independence 22–3
Internal control *see* controls, internal
Introducing statistical sampling 115–19

Judgmental sampling *see* sampling

Key items 56
  control questions (KCQ) 93
  see also controls, internal

Manual selection 42–3, 58, 70, 75
Materiality 67–8, 143
  see also safety margin
Maximum tolerable error 45, 148
Mean per unit sample *see* sampling
Monetary unit sample *see* sampling
  initial precautions 55–6

Nightmare scenarios 91–3
Non statistical sampling *see* sampling
Normal distribution, the 30–31

Objectives 90–91, 151

Options, two 67–8

Pitfalls 25–6, 53–6
Planning 25
  see also introducing statistical
    sampling
Poisson distribution 33–4
Point estimate *see* precision
Population 34–6, 151–52
  characteristics 35
Precision 31–2, 61–3, 141–42
  basic 69
  gap widening (PGW) 68–70
Probability 14, 29–30
  proportional to size (PPS) 52–5, 144
Professional standards 17–19

Randomness 37, 42–3, 155
Ratio estimation 112
Reliability factor 33–4, 42, 96
  allocation of 100–101, 109, 131–38
Risk models 87–105
  control 94–6
  detection 94–6
  inherent 94–6
  key 91–3
  see also confidence

Safety margin 67–70
  see also materiality
Sample size 8–9, 40, 52, 54, 61, 99–101,
    109–11, 152–54, 158–60

Sampling
  acceptance 107–10
  attribute 39–50
  equal interval 13–14, 155
  frames 35
  haphazard 11–12, 155
  interval 40–41, 63–4
    see also equal interval
  judgmental 12–13
  mean per unit 111–12
  monetary unit 51–85
  non statistical 7–10
  risk 152–54
  statistical 14–15, 155
  unit 35, 54
  variables 111–13
Skills 25–6
  see also introducing statistical
    sampling
Standard deviation 112–13
Substantive test *see* testing

Tainting 71
Testing, audit 19–22, 116
  compliance 51–2
  substantive 52–3

Upper error limit (UEL) 54, 110, 146
  see also precision

Variables sampling *see* sampling

Working papers, example 72–3

Printed in Great Britain
by Amazon

44210747R00106